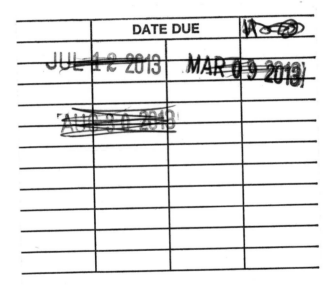

DON'T
SIT
ON
THE
BABY

1 |13
1 2 99

First published in 2012 by Zest Books
35 Stillman Street, Suite 121, San Francisco, CA 94107
www.zestbooks.net
Created and produced by Zest Books, San Francisco, CA

Typeset in Sabon and Gill Sans

Teen Nonfiction / Careers / Babysitting

Library of Congress Control Number: 2011942757
ISBN: 978-0-9827322-3-6

CREDITS
BOOK EDITOR: Rebecca Frazer
CREATIVE DIRECTOR: Hallie Warshaw
ART DIRECTOR/COVER DESIGN: Tanya Napier
GRAPHIC DESIGN: Marissa Feind
MANAGING EDITOR/ PRODUCTION EDITOR: Pam McElroy
RESEARCH EDITOR: Nikki Roddy
INTERN: Alice Dalrymple

TEEN ADVISORS: Amelia Alvarez, Ema Barnes, Anna Livia Chen, Huitzi Herrera-Sobal, and Felicity Massa

Manufactured in China
LEO 10 9 8 7 6 5 4 3 2 1
4500345835

Every effort has been made to ensure that the information presented is accurate. The publisher disclaims any liability for injuries, losses, untoward results, or any other damages that may result from the use of the information in this book.

DON'T

SIT
ON
THE
BABY

**The Ultimate Guide to Sane,
Skilled, and Safe Babysitting**

Halley Bondy

INTRODUCTION

So you're thinking about babysitting. You love kids, you need the cash, and you've got a little free time. Luckily there are tons of opportunities for a fun, entrepreneurial teen like you. Even beginners can enter the babysitting force with plenty of time to spare for school and socializing. It's a great way to build your résumé and earn money for the awesome stuff your parents won't buy—and you get to play hide-and-seek while you're at it!

But all perks aside, babysitting is no cakewalk. After all, if kids weren't a lot of work, sitters wouldn't exist. Children need to be fed, clothed, put to bed, consoled, changed, and most of all, they need to feel safe in your care. As an added challenge, kids can be unpredictable, rowdy, and defiant. (Remember all those tantrums you threw as a child? Prepare for swift retribution!) Depending on the kids' ages, the number of children, and their personalities, the pressure can get pretty intense. Not to mention, when it's all over, you have to wear a smile for the parents—even if you spent an hour scraping macaroni from the ceiling!

With all these demands in your midst, it's important to remember that no sitter is perfect. All parents and sitters make mistakes sometimes (in fact, they'll be the first to tell you that Mary Poppins doesn't exist!). But if you picked up this book, it means that you're ready to accept the challenge, learn from your mistakes, and accept new, crucial tips.

In the following pages, you'll learn how to deal with the most difficult babysitting experiences. You'll take a quiz to determine what type of babysitting job suits your needs. You'll learn the ins and outs of a sitter's responsibilities, from diapers to dinner to bedtime. You'll also learn some babysitting essentials, like how to react in emergency situations, how to play like a kid again, and how to keep a screaming child from driving you nuts. You'll even read some fun firsthand babysitting stories from teens like you!

On the business side, you'll learn how to deal with your rate, how to maneuver the job market, and how to gauge your strengths and weaknesses so you don't feel in over your head. You'll even learn how to take your babysitting expertise to new professional heights.

Most of all, you'll learn how to have fun on the job. After all, you chose this noble profession because kids are the most entertaining, rewarding, and adorable creatures to be around. These little ones need you, and the more prepared you are, the better the job will be for both of you!

Now get out there and sit (But never, ever on the baby)!

CONTENTS 🍽

BUSINESS BASICS

A

BABYSITTING

BREAKDOWN

1. WHAT IS BABYSITTING?

Babysitting is a misleading job title. According to our friends at *Webster*, babysitting has nothing to do with sitting on babies. A babysitter is a person hired to care for children when parents are not home. Babysitting is one of the most popular gigs for teens around— despite all the responsibility, frustration, and booger cleaning! Even better, babysitting doesn't require filling out a lengthy application or a formal interview process. And you can find potential clients in your family, through friends, and in your neighborhood. If you have younger siblings or cousins, you already have experience! And, possibly the best part of entering the world of babysitting? It's one of those jobs that never go away: As long as there are busy parents in the world, babysitters will have a job caring for their kids.

"Sitting" (as the pros call it) has been around for ages and is a far better job than it used to be. Years ago, in the Victorian Age, nannies were typically poor women filling in as parents for rich families. They often started working when they were incredibly young, were treated like servants at best, and spent more time with the kids than the parents did. But times have changed. These days, parents respect sitters for all their hard work and trust their little loved one's well-being in the care of a sitter.

But while babysitting has evolved over the years, the main goal remains the same: to make sure the child stays happy, healthy, and safe in your care. This means making sure the child doesn't watch violent TV shows or gorge on candy, and is returned to the parents in one piece at the end of the day or evening. Babysitting has often been brushed off as an easy job, but it's not easy, and it's certainly not trivial. Remember, someone's safety is in your hands.

It's a Tough Job

You may have heard that babysitting is easy and that anyone can do it, but that's a myth—babysitting is hard work. Kids fall down. Kitchens catch fire. Parents come home three hours later than they said they would. And sometimes, no matter how much you do to keep the kids happy and entertained, they just won't stop freaking out. How can you make it stop without tearing out your last hair?

Nobody is born with complete childcare know-how. To babysit, you need skills. Not just basic childcare skills, either. You need patience, intelligence, and a great sense of humor. After all, it takes some quick wit to convince Tommy that the toilet isn't trying to eat him. You have a little life in your hands (no matter how stubborn he may be), so everything counts, from your in-control attitude to your negotiating skills, all the way down to your friendly smile.

So, What's In It for You?

Why babysit instead of, say, stock groceries? For one, as a babysitter, you'll have more control over your salary and schedule than other jobs available to you (see "Business Basics"). You'll also have access to television, books, and comfy furniture. But the rewards go beyond the simple perks. Babysitting can be deeply gratifying. It's a highly creative job. You have to think on your feet and constantly come up with new ways to keep a kid safe and entertained. Plus, not too many jobs offer the rush of seeing a toddler walk for the first time or helping a 3rd grader ace a test she was really nervous about. Those are priceless moments, and you won't get those kinds of perks in the produce aisle. Kids often remember their babysitters forever, so think about the impact a babysitter can make on future generations. It's hardly something to scoff at!

2. WHAT KIND OF SITTER ARE YOU?

Love singing nursery rhymes, playing board games, and helping with homework? Then babysitting could be the perfect gig for you. But be warned, not everyone is cut out for childcare. Take this quiz to find out if you really have what it takes.

1. Your energy level is:
A. Way too high, I'm told.
B. I've got a few good hours in me.
C. Can I get a Red Bull before answering that?

2. Your niceness level is:
A. Off the charts.
B. I'm nice, especially to kids.
C. I'm sort of nice, until someone annoys me.

3. Your cleaning habits are:
A. Persnickety. I can't stand messes.
B. Moderate. I clean when I must.
C. What? I don't even notice messes.

4. You are certified in:
A. CPR, First Aid, and/or Red Cross babysitting classes.
B. Nothing, but I have a basic knowledge of CPR, the Heimlich maneuver, and First Aid.
C. R&R. Is there a certificate for that?

5. Drool and snot are:
A. Fun!
B. A part of life.
C. Totally gross.

6. Cooking is:

A. My specialty!

B. I can use a microwave.

C. Boring. Takeout for me, thanks.

7. Your teaching skills are:

A. Masterful. I can turn any kid into a prodigy.

B. Average. I can teach a subject or two.

C. Nil. I hate explaining things.

**8. If you had to pick games
to play with a kid, they would be:**

A. Dolls, house, and hide-and-seek.

B. Video games or board games.

C. The quiet game.

9. When an emergency strikes, you:

A. Call 911, use my emergency training if applicable,
then call the parents.

B. Call 911, then call the parents.

C. Panic, yell, and hope the whole thing blows over.

10. When you get angry, you:

A. Take a few deep breaths and try to approach the problem calmly.

B. Swallow it, smile, and scream when I'm in private.

C. Yell until I get my way.

Find out here what kind of babysitter you are (or aren't):

If you answered mostly As: Are you serious? Nobody likes diapers and drool! Are you some kind of a babysitting android? Your energy level, patience, and overall childcare smarts make you a natural fit for kids of all ages. With your shining personality and résumé, you'll definitely land a few jobs. However, your passion can be a little overwhelming for some kids and parents. Try to relax sometimes and allow yourself to make mistakes. You're only human!

Mostly Bs: What you lack in professional cred, you make up for in open-mindedness, versatility, common sense, and a can-do attitude. You're eager, capable, and probably ready to hit the job hunt, but it might be better to practice on older kids or family members first. They're (usually) lower maintenance.

Mostly Cs: You may want to consider a retail job. Kids drive you nuts and taking care of them is the last thing you want to spend your free time doing. But hey—that's OK. Babysitting is not for everyone.

3. TYPES OF JOBS TO SUIT YOUR SCHEDULE

You're searching online for a babysitting job, and you come across the gig of your dreams. Responsibilities include: watching television, raiding the fridge, and surfing the web until the parents come home. There's only one kid, and he spends most of his time in his room studying. The job pays, or it might as well, a bajillion dollars an hour. Oh, and you'd get free reign over their swimming pool.

Did somebody say jackpot?! Only . . . there's one teensy issue. It's practically a full-time job. You would need to babysit everyday after school for five hours—plus weekends.

Ever an ambitious person, you wrestle with yourself.

Can I squeeze in the time? Maybe if I drop out of swim team, scramble to finish all of my homework on the bus, and study for tests during lunchtime. Or . . . or . . .

Hold it right there, Superman.

Be realistic. There's no way you can sustain a job when you don't have the time. You need to pick the type of job that suits your needs (not to mention, your threshold for the work). Unfortunately, this may mean letting a few fantasy jobs slide. It's not a great feeling, but school and extracurricular activities should always come first. Don't worry, there's always another job around the corner!

There are several types of babysitting jobs, and each comes with its own set of hours and responsibilities. Below are some of the most common babysitting jobs you'll encounter. Choose wisely!

After-School or Nighttime Sitter

A lot of parents need babysitters while they're finishing work or when they have evening plans, so after-school and nighttime sitters are in high demand. This kind of job would require some juggling on your part. After all, you likely have your own after-school responsibilities to deal with. With this job type, you may have to pick up the kids from school, wait for them at a bus stop, or thank their carpool driver. If they're busy like most kids, they may need an escort to soccer practice or play dates. When the parents are out late, you may have to make dinner and put the kids to bed.

Weekend Sitter

If you're a full-time student—and have swim practice every day after school— a weekend babysitting job might be just right for you. You wouldn't arrive exhausted after a day of school, and you could still leave plenty of time for weekend fun. Like all babysitting jobs,  the responsibilities of a weekend sitter depend on the kid's age and needs, but they'll likely involve prescheduled weekend activities, like play dates, soccer games, music lessons, or theater classes. You may need to escort them to and from these events, or if the event calls for it, you may need to be their cheerleader.

Overnight Sitter

Parents go on business trips (or even vacations) without their little ones, so they need someone they can trust to rule the roost overnight. The duties of a part-time overnight sitter include the full range of childcare, from waking kids up in the morning to getting them wherever they need to go to putting them to bed at night (and then maybe doing it all over again the next day). Babysitters who spend the night naturally have to deal with bedtime drama, like nightmares and bedwetting, followed by morning chores like preparing breakfast. Overnight sitters should have some extra emergency training, since they're watching the kids (not to mention the house and the pets) for such a huge chunk of time. It's a big responsibility, so parents will usually hire experienced sitters for these positions.

Summer Sitter

If you don't want to sit on the couch this summer, it might be a great time to babysit! If your schedule is wide open, you could use the time to earn lots of cash (and add some points on your résumé). There's plenty of demand for full-time summer babysitters for five or more days a week, because most parents still have to work. Other families bring babysitters along for vacation, which could mean a free trip to the beach for you! It could also mean watching over the kid in a foreign environment, so summer sitters should be confident and adaptable.

With so many kinds of babysitting jobs out there, there's sure to be one that's right for you. Be realistic with yourself about your schedule, abilities, and patience level, and you'll find your match!

4. WHAT TO EXPECT FROM KIDS 0 TO 10

Kids come in a variety of ages, and each age requires a different level and type of care. As a babysitter, you'll need to decide what age group you're most comfortable with so that you can narrow down your job hunt. Not sure? This quick breakdown will clue you in on the personality traits and skills you'll need to care for kids ages 0 to 10. And don't forget to wash your hands before you care for any kid!

Newborns (0 to 3 Months Old)

What They're Like

✔ These tiny creatures can hardly move, support their own heads, or hold their own bottles.

✔ They need a good dose of formula or pumped breast milk around every two to three hours, or they may start crying hysterically.

✔ The good news: Newborns sleep for sixteen hours a day at two to three hour intervals.

✔ The bad news: You're looking at full-on diaper duty.

What You'll Need

✔ A gentle touch and a desire to be really, really needed. Newborns are fragile (their bones haven't fully developed yet), and you'll be carrying them a lot.

✔ Decoding skills. Cracking the newborn language code isn't easy. They don't cry only when they're hungry. Maybe the little booger already ate and needs to be burped. Or maybe she's uncomfortable and needs a diaper change, an extra sweater, or a good rocking session. It's your job to figure it out.

✔ Maturity. In general, you shouldn't babysit for a newborn until you're at least fourteen years old, or until you have plenty of experience.

Infants (4 to 11 Months Old)

What They're Like

✔ These kids are starting to crawl, sit, and eventually walk (with your help!).

✔ Younger infants are probably learning how to hold their own bottles, while older ones are likely eating mushy stuff (like baby food) on top of their scheduled feedings. If they can support their own heads and necks, they can sit in a high chair during meals.

✔ Diapers are still the norm.

✔ Infants will usually sleep multiple times a day for hours at a time.

✔ An infant's jibber-jabber may help you figure out why she's crying.

✔ Infants start teething at six months old, which means you're in for a lot of drooling, chewing, and crankiness.

✔ They also start to feel separation anxiety at about eight months old, which means they may fuss and cry for a while after their parents leave.

What You'll Need

✔ A cautious eye to make sure that the kids don't sidle up next to sharp things.

✔ Plenty of cleaning materials nearby, since food and drool will get everywhere.

✔ A patient attitude. It's easy to get frustrated when the kids take a long time to finish their mush, or when you can't stop the crying right away.

Toddlers (1 to 2 Years Old)

What They're Like

✔ These kids can move. Fast. This is not always fun in the middle of a diaper change or dinner, or when there are safety hazards (like stairs) involved, but they will give you a great workout!

✔ Toddlers can usually drink out of covered cups and eat solid food with their hands (have cleaning supplies handy).

✔ They sleep for about ten to thirteen hours at night.

✔ They'll likely still need diapers, though some early birds start potty-training at this age.

✔ They should be able to tell you (even if it's in their own special language) that they need to be changed.

✔ The littlest things can become cataclysmic whinefests. (There's a reason they call it the Terrible Twos.)

What You'll Need

✔ A lot of patience. These kids want to assert their independence, and sometimes the best way they know how to do that is with a tantrum.

✔ The ability to take a deep breath, use a calm tone of voice, and not react from your gut immediately.

✔ Lots of extra energy, since these kids are starting to get into active games, like tag or finding hidden objects.

Preschoolers (3 to 4 Years Old)

What They're Like

✔ Preschoolers can walk and run on their own, though they'll need to hold your hand sometimes, especially when crossing the street.

✔ By this age, kids are typically potty-training with adult assistance, and they may wear diapers at night.

✔ These kids need supervision in the tub, and they probably need help getting cleaned and dressed.

✔ These kids can tell you when they're hungry and what they want to eat, and they are learning to feed themselves with regular utensils.

✔ They can be really picky, and mealtime can drag on due to an endless number of delaying tactics (theirs, not yours).

✔ Some of these kids will do anything to not face bedtime, and when they do go to sleep, they may have nightmares!

What You'll Need

✔ A lot of creativity (and maybe your old Halloween costumes). Preschoolers love make-believe games. They also love books, though they won't know how to read for a few more years.

✔ Patience. You'll need to be flexible, since they often get stubborn or defiant.

✔ An arsenal of lullabies. While they sleep for about ten to twelve hours at night, four-year-olds may have a nasty case of nightmares and will need you to help lull them back to sleep.

Kindergarteners to 2nd Graders (5 to 7 Years Old)

What They're Like

✔ My, my, they grow up so fast! These kids can pretty much take care of the basics—dressing, eating, and bathing—by themselves, so you probably won't need to chase them down too much. Unless, of course, you're playing tag.

✔ They may still need help with more advanced tasks like cutting, drawing, and reading, but that's the fun part.

✔ Kindergarteners may still be picky about what food they eat, but they can eat regular meals without your help (and they probably don't want your help either).

✔ They should be able to go to the bathroom and take a bath without your help (though you should always supervise bath time just in case).

✔ At night, there might be some rare cases of bedwetting. If you're grossed out, try your best to not freak out.

What You'll Need

✔ Stellar negotiating tactics. By now the kids can speak totally clearly, and they've also learned how to use words to their advantage. Though serious tantrums should have stopped, these kids may still put up a fight (or worse, lie to you) about things like bed time, homework, and their snack allowance.

✔ Creative cooking skills. Kids this age tend to be picky eaters.

3rd to 5th Graders (8 to 10 Years Old)

What They're Like

✔ These kids are more or less independent and biding time before they don't need a babysitter.

✔ You'll probably still need to cook or order food for them, but they can at least help around the kitchen.

✔ If you do need to chase them down for anything, it will likely be to do their homework (which they might need your help with). Better brush up on that long division!

What You'll Need

✔ Flexibility and an open mind. Older children can communicate very clearly, and they're forming an independent, critical point of view. In other words, they might be know-it-alls.

✔ They're pretty much up to their own thing, so you'll need to figure out when to stay out of their way (i.e., if they have a trusted friend over and they'd like to play a game without you—of course you'll still be keeping an eye on them) and when to intervene (i.e., if they're online when they're not supposed to be).

Special Needs Kids

The term "special needs" refers to just about every disability out there, ranging from attention deficit disorder to autism to physical paralysis. Like all kids, no two special needs kids are alike, and disabilities can range from mild to severe. Their health, their behavior, and their schoolwork may be heavily impacted, or not affected at all. Chances are, parents will only hire older, experienced babysitters to watch over a severely impaired child. If you're interested in learning about caring for special needs kids, you can visit Childcare.gov, or volunteer at your local community centers, libraries, and schools.

5. GETTING STARTED

So, you've taken a quiz, worked out how many free hours you have in your schedule, and mulled over your tolerance for diapers. You're pretty confident in your babysitting skills. But do you really have what it takes? Maybe, but you don't want to test your new knowledge after the parents leave you alone with three screaming kids and a sea of baby formula!

If you walk into a babysitting job cold, you may be overwhelmed by surprises. Maybe you don't realize how hectic it can be when there are kids around, how loud kids can cry, or how stubborn they get over small things. The hard reality of babysitting is a lot different than it is in a book.

So before you start a babysitting job, practice on some real live kids in a less urgent environment. Get to know them. Test your game skills, your tantrum strategies, your homework help, your cooking abilities—whatever you think may be challenging on the job.

But where do you find your guinea pigs? Read below. (If you already have experience with children, feel free to skip to the next chapter!)

Go for the sibling. You may already have a little brother or sister, in which case, you know perfectly well what a handful little kids can be. But you could still improve your babysitting skills by helping your parents with the rough stuff once in a while.
Volunteer to cook dinner for your little sister tonight. Try introducing new games into the fold. If she starts throwing a minor fit, try

resolving the issue without getting Mom. These are all skills that you need in a babysitting situation, so why not start at home?

Talk to neighbors, family friends, or relatives. You could ask trusted relatives or friends to let you hang around their kids (with adults around) for experience. If you go to the movies with your family, for example, you can practice things like escorting the kids to the bathroom or buckling them in a car seat on the way home. Parents are always grateful for the help!

Babysit while parents are home. Some parents need babysitters while they're still in the house. Maybe they work from home, or maybe they just need an extra hand. Whatever the reason, this can be a great way to gain experience and maybe even make some money.

Volunteer. You don't have to go to a house to get experience with kids. You can also volunteer at local schools, summer camps, religious centers, libraries, museums, daycare centers, neighborhood associations—you get the picture. Often, these kinds of institutions take young volunteers to help run family events, like block parties or field trips.

Get a mentor. Know somebody who has some babysitting experience? Don't be afraid to ask them for advice. After all, they were once in your shoes.

ESSENTIAL

SKILLS

6. FEEDING HUNGRY MOUTHS

It seems so simple. Food goes in mouth. Mouth chews food. Food gets swallowed. The end. Right? So, why is Sally using her macaroni as a telescope? And why does she cry when the vegetables touch the meat? And on what planet are gummy bears a meal?!

These questions have been confounding adults the world over, and there are simply no answers. Kids are the world's freakiest, most puzzling eaters. But while it's not worth probing the logic behind those celestial macaronis, as a babysitter, you still have to ensure that your young charges eat.

During meals, you have to deal with cooking, messes, picky eaters, bottles, and delicate tummies. Food requirements will vary depending on the ages of the children (see page 20), the time you babysit (see page 17), and the kids' tastes.

Below are tips to help make meal times easier. Remember, you should always get the full rundown from the parents on dietary restrictions (think vegetarian instead of meat, or a child with a peanut or other food allergy) and any religious or cultural customs (think chopsticks instead of knives and forks, or maybe it's Ramadan, Passover, or Lent).

Bottle Feeding Basics

If you're babysitting for infants or toddlers, you'll probably have to deal with baby bottles. Giving a baby a bottle may seem like an easy, two-step process: you fill the bottle and feed the kid. But there are actually a number of things to think about, like what to put in the bottle, what temperature the liquid should be, and how to hold the baby so he doesn't choke. While older infants and toddlers may be able to feed themselves (with a little help from you), a baby is way too young to hold a bottle on her own. Below are some best practices you can employ to ensure a successful feeding session.

① **Sterilize everything.** Bottles, bottle nipples, caps, and rings need to be squeaky clean. Otherwise, the baby can get sick from germs. If the bottles and accessories are new, boil them in water for five minutes and cool them completely before you use them. If they've been used before, wash them with soap, water, and a clean bottle brush.

② **Fill the bottle.** Bottles can be filled with pumped breast milk or baby formula, depending on the age of the child and the feeding preferences of the parents. Mom and Dad should have already given you specific instructions, but here are some additional pointers for each liquid:

- *Breast milk.* Refrigerated breast milk goes bad after two or three days, while frozen breast milk goes bad after two weeks. Most moms will have dates on the bottles, so check those and use the older, but not expired, ones first. Some parents are extra careful about contamination, and they'll ask you to throw away any leftover breast milk after one feeding. If not, then store the leftover breast milk in the fridge or freezer between feeding times.

- *Baby formula.* You may have to mix powdered formula with water (the water should be boiled and cooled), or the drink may be ready-made. In any case, follow the instructions on the packaging, and strictly abide by the expiration date. Ready-made formula usually stays edible for forty-eight hours after opening as long as it's stored in the fridge; you shouldn't store powdered formula after it has been mixed as it may get clumpy.

③ **Test the temperature.** If the parents tell you to warm the milk or formula before feeding, you can't just pop it in the microwave or warm it up on a stove. You'll burn the kid's mouth, and you may even change the chemicals in the food. Instead, fill the bottle with the liquid food and run it under a warm tap. Shake it well and test the temperature by putting a drop on your wrist. The drop should be closer to room temperature than to boiling, and it shouldn't leave a pink mark on your wrist. If it does, it's still too hot!

④ **Prep the baby.** Loosely tie or velcro a clean bib around the baby's neck. Also have a clean, soft cloth handy to wipe up any messes. Hold the bottle with one hand, and hold the baby close to you with the other. (He should be in a slightly upright position, with his head higher than his body.) Make sure both you and the baby are comfortable, because you could be in this position for a while.

⑤ **Start the bottle feeding.** Hold the bottle upside down until the nipple fills with milk. You want the baby to swallow as little air as possible, or you'll pay for it during burp time when he lets out a stinky, milky belch. Tap the tip of the nipple against the baby's lips. He should respond by putting it in his mouth. As the baby sucks on the bottle, look for little bubbles rising from the nipple. If you don't see bubbles, the milk may not be flowing out. Make sure the nipple isn't clogged or that the nipple hasn't collapsed (that is, sucked in toward the bottle). Both of these problems may be helped by loosening the top slightly.

6 **Look for spit-up.** Spit-up is a cute way of saying "a little puke." Babies' digestive systems aren't fully developed yet, so they'll spit up after they eat. This is totally normal. Just use the cloth to wipe up the baby's mouth. You should only be concerned if the children projectile vomit, or they vomit in brown or green, which could be bile or blood, not milk. If this happens, call the parents immediately.

7 **Take a burp break.** Swallowing air is an unavoidable part of bottle feeding. And it can be pretty irritating for an infant. (It can also increase their spit-up.) This is why it's important to burp a baby after he drinks about two to three ounces. When you burp a child, hold him close to your chest while supporting his neck with one hand and letting his chin rest on your shoulder. Repeatedly pat his back (lightly!) until he lets out a nice, healthy belch. Just make sure that you've got a towel under his chin or on your shoulder to catch any surprise spit-up.

8 **Know when to stop.** The baby may be finished (or may be taking a break) when he closes his mouth, stops sucking, or turns away from the nipple. If you already burped him and he doesn't continue eating, he's probably full. But if he rejects food for hours, there may be a problem, so be sure to inform the parents immediately.

SAFETY FIRST!

Q. *What do I do if a child is choking?*

A. **If a child aged one year or older is choking (meaning they swallowed something and they can't cough, breathe, or make noise) you should perform the Heimlich maneuver. To do this:**

1. Kneel behind the child, wrap your arms around his waist, and place the thumb part of your fist against the child's stomach, between his navel and his sternum.

2. Wrap your other hand around your fist, and thrust quickly in an inward, upward motion; make sure to be gentle with little kids.

3. Thrust until the food pops out of his mouth, or until he faints. If he does faint, call 911 and start performing cardiopulmonary resuscitation (aka CPR) (see page 66 to find out how).

A. If the child is less than one year old:

If you are ever in doubt about what to do, or how to do it, always **call 911** at any time.

1. Place the baby face down on your forearm, using your thigh for support.

2. Hold his head lower than his body, and be sure to support his head gently with your hand.

3. Slap the baby forcefully between his shoulder blades five times. If the food or object doesn't come out by the fifth blow, turn the infant face up and lay him on your lap to keep his head supported.

4. Place two fingers on the middle of his breastbone, and give five quick thrusts down, compressing the chest, but not too hard.

5. Alternate between the back slaps and chest thrusts until the object comes out. If the baby goes unconscious, call 911 after one minute of infant CPR (see page 66 to find out how). If you're able to see the object in his throat, you may be able to remove it with your finger, but only do this if it's in plain sight.*

* Instructions taken from the American Heart Association 2005 American Heart Association guidelines for cardiopulmonary resuscitation and emergency cardiovascular care: Part 3: Overview of CPR.

Baby Food Rules

Baby food is like grown-up food, only a lot mushier. Most kids can start eating baby food when they're between four and six months old, though it's really up to the parents. Some parents will want you to give their kids baby food in addition to breast milk or formula in bottles or covered sippy cups. Others may tell you to stick to baby food alone. If parents prefer homemade concoctions like mashed-up rice cereal or puréed vegetables, meat, and fruit versus ready-to-eat baby food from a jar, they should prepare it for you. Or, make sure they at least give you thorough instructions on how to cook and store the food so you can prep it yourself. Ready to eat? Here are some quick tips to get you started.

① **Prep for mealtime.** Just like with bottle feeding, you want to wash your hands and put a bib on the kid. If he's old enough to sit in a high chair, you want to make sure he's buckled securely in place. (Don't use a high chair until the parents show you how.) You can also spoon-feed the child while holding him upright on your lap. Make sure you have a clean cloth handy!

② **Let them play.** Children may attempt to eat with their hands. This is totally normal, and will take some patience on your part. They may want to hurl their food around or use it as a toy. If they're still discovering finger food, you should tolerate play. You can cajole them into taking an occasional bite by pretending to eat it, too.

③ **Accept the mess.** Food that falls on the floor is a lost cause, and a natural part of baby feeding. Same with all those dribbles on the bib. However, you may be able to save the food that winds up on a baby's chin and lips. Just scrape the stray food with a baby-friendly rubber-covered spoon, pretend the spoon is an airplane, and put it into his mouth.

Cooking for Picky Kids

Some kids love simple foods like sandwiches, but if you don't cut them diagonally, they may lose their appetite completely. Other kids feel it's their moral obligation to resist eating anything that even resembles a green vegetable. Whatever the kid's issue is, it's not an insult to your culinary genius. Pickiness is a natural, random, annoying phenomenon that generations of babysitters have had to deal with. If a kid throws your finest stew against the wall, don't take it personally. Instead, follow these tips.

① **Stick to the parents' routine.** Try not to introduce new food to picky eaters right away. It's better to stick to the parents' menu. Once you get accustomed to the kid, you can start being more spontaneous. Until then, keep that tuna meat-cheese-celery surprise (or any surprise for that matter) on the backburner.

② **Make food awesome.** Food looks a lot more interesting when it's in the shape of a smiley face, when it's part of a theme night (orange-colored dinner night?), or when you accompany every successful bite with a funny song. Make healthy food appealing by adding a kid-friendly touch (yogurt with sprinkles, anyone?). Turn to page 40 for two awesome recipe ideas.

③ **Avoid bribing.** A lot of people haggle with kids to make them eat. A common tactic is saying, "Eat five more string beans and you'll get dessert," or, "Drink your milk and then you can play video games." These seem like reasonable trades, but experts don't recommend this kind of bribery. Children will start to see food as one big power struggle. They'll notice that the food issue gets under your skin and that they can use it to get what they want.

TALES FROM THE CRIB

I remember a time when I was babysitting for my seven-year-old younger brother and he complained of being hungry. I had no idea what to make him, but I had a lot of bravado. So, I asked, "Do you want something out of the box or a can?" He told me he wanted a sandwich. OK, easy enough! I then asked, "Do you want ham? Do you want jelly?" He wrinkled his nose and said, "Jelly is gross!" I asked, "How about tuna?" He said, "Fish is icky!" (Mind you, he had never tried fish in his life.) We went back and forth a few more times before he said, "I want peanut butter." Then we had to decide what kind of peanut butter: smooth or chunky. When we got to the bread, he said he wanted it cut into triangles. Finally, I was done: I had chunky peanut butter on triangle-shaped bread—a forty-minute adventure!

—Jessie G., 15

④ **Get rid of distractions.** Sometimes kids will decline food, not because they're full, but because they've got one eye on the cartoons in the next room. Before mealtime, you should turn off the TV and put away the toys so the kids can focus on eating.

⑤ **Let their apppetite speak.** Kids know when they're hungry, and they know when they're full. You don't want to force feed kids, you don't want to rush them, and you don't want to pressure them to make sure they eat every crumb. Your job is to make sure that the kids eat enough healthy food to tide them over before their parents come home. This is a lot easier if you pay attention to the kids' actual hunger levels. If they're still just not eating, try another tactic on this list.

⑥ **Eat with the kids.** This makes eating more of a bonding experience for the kids instead of a lonely chore. It may also encourage them to eat. They may take your example and try to imitate your impressive fork skills.

⑦ **Let them help.** Children are more likely to enjoy mealtime if they have a part in it. If they're old enough, allow the kids to help you cook, set the table, or wash dishes, and then praise them for a job well done. Obviously, never let a child handle boiling water, scalding surfaces, or sharp knives on your watch. The point is to make mealtime a fun, tear-free bonding experience.

Here are two easy recipes that are sure to please many kids.

Kiddie Veggie Kebabs
(For Children Ages 6 and Up)

You Need
1 box of wooden BBQ sticks
1 celery stalk per child
5 baby carrots
5 cherry tomatoes per child
1 cup ranch dip

Chop the bigger veggies into bite-size pieces, and arrange them on a plate. If the kids are old enough, about seven and up, let them stick the food with the clean BBQ sticks (or do it for them). Just be careful, these sticks are usually sharp, so supervise the children at all times, and warn them not to touch the pointy end. Also, keep in mind that other food can be used to make a kebab, too. So if you don't have the veggies listed, try bite-size pieces of fruit or pieces of penne pasta and cheese.

Green Eggs and Ham
(For Children Ages 4 and Up)

No, Dr. Seuss didn't make them up. You can actually make this delightful delicacy with the power of eggs, ham, and magic (or food coloring).

You Need
2 eggs per child
½ to 1 slice of ham per child
Green food coloring
1 tbsp butter or olive oil

First, cook the ham (without the help of the children). To do this, turn the stove on low. Melt some butter or heat olive oil in a frying pan. Put the ham in the pan, and wait until the slices become slightly crispy (but not burned) on both sides. When you think the ham is done, turn off the stove and set the ham aside. Now, cook the eggs. Let the kids try cracking all the eggs into a big bowl. Have them beat the eggs with a fork or wisk until the liquid is all yellow. Ask the kids to add a few drops of green food dye to the egg batter while you (or another sibling) continue beating it. Watch them stare in awe as the egg batter turns green! Set the food dye aside, and ask the children to step away from the stove. Turn on the stove, melt butter or heat a few drops of olive oil in a frying pan, and pour the eggs into the pan. You make green scrambled eggs by moving the eggs around the pan with a spatula until there's no more liquid egg left. The eggs should be the consistency of mashed potatoes: not too runny, not too hard. Place the ham next to the eggs on a plate, and *voila*! You've made Dr. Seuss proud.

7. DEALING WITH DIAPERS AND POTTIES

You've got a two-month-old baby on your lap, and things start to stink. (Didn't you just change her?) Knowing full well that unmentionable things are happening on your jeans, you rush to the diaper changing table, wipes at the ready. But when you open the diaper, it's totally clean. Relieved but baffled, you return to the couch.

Five minutes later, the stench picks up again. Once more, you run to the changing table. Clean diaper. And again. Clean diaper. You sit back down and crank up the TV volume. The stink intensifies, but by now you've learned your lesson. You don't budge. And of course, that's when the unmentionable *really* happens. Worse— by now, the diaper is so loose from all that fastening and unfastening, it couldn't contain the avalanche. You, babysitter, like so many babysitters before you, are covered in poop.

Diapers and toilet training are stinky, unfortunate realities of baby-sitting little kids. Until they are fully potty trained, you have to do a lot of the dirty work for them. It's an icky job, but if you're not on top of it, things will get a whole lot ickier.

Changing Diapers

Babies eat all the time, which means they poop and pee all the time, too. You can usually tell it's time for a diaper change by the stench. But as the scenario above shows, the baby may just be fussy and gassy. If it's been about two to three hours since her last diaper change, you'll want to take a peek.
Toddlers may even be able to tell you they need a diaper clean-up. When the time comes, wash your hands, and then follow these simple instructions.

① Prepare everything you need. Before the parents leave, find out where everything is located: baby wipes; clean diapers; a soft, clean cloth for the baby to lie on; some plastic bags for storing dirty clothes; and, if necessary, a change of clothes for the baby.

② Most parents use a specific changing table, where they stock all their supplies. Lay the baby on her back on a changing table or other designated clean, flat surface. (Never leave a baby unsupervised. She could roll over and fall.)

③ Remove the baby's bottom clothes and the dirty diaper. Most diapers have sticky tabs on both sides. Peel off each tab, lift the baby's legs with one hand, and slide the dirty diaper out with the other hand.

④ Throw the dirty diaper away in the diaper bin, or, if there is none, the trash can. (Make sure you don't toss it in the family laundry hamper by accident.)

⑤ Lift the child's legs again, and use baby wipes to clean her bottom and privates. (Always wipe girls from front to back.) Throw away the dirty diaper wipes before you move on.

⑥ Grab the clean diaper, and open it. Lift the baby by her legs again and slide the diaper under her bum. The wider side (where the sticky tabs are) should be on the bottom.

⑦ Latch the front and back of the diaper together with the sticky tabs on the sides. Make sure the latch is on securely to avoid any avalanches! Put the baby's clothes on, and you're done. Don't forget to wash your hands again!

Potty Training

Believe it or not, toilets can be trickier than diapers. Diapers offer a nice safeguard against disasters, but kids who are just learning how to use a toilet can have accidents at any time. And there's never a good time for an accident. You can minimize mishaps by gently encouraging kids to go to the bathroom as much as possible, especially before they leave the house, after every meal, and before they go to bed. If you spot them clutching their pants, fidgeting, or just looking really uncomfortable, know that those are telltale signs that they have to use the toilet. Here's what to do when you get there.

SAFETY FIRST!

Q: How do I deal with and avoid diaper rash?

A: Diaper rash is an irritation of any skin covered by the diaper, often caused by build-ups of bacteria or yeast that love moist environments like babies' diapers. You can tell when a baby has diaper rash by big red splotches and inflamed scaly skin located anywhere on the skin inside the diaper. It's easy to treat by applying creams to the infected area, but if diaper rash gets too out of control, it can lead to a more serious infection. Ask the parents what cream (if any) you should use. To prevent diaper rash, you should keep the area as dry as you can. Change her diapers every two to three hours. Wrap the diaper loosely so there's air traveling inside, and don't use any harsh soaps when you wash the child.

① Put a potty-training seat on the toilet bowl, if necessary. This is a small booster seat that saves the kid from falling into the toilet. Sometimes, the children may even use miniature potties while they train. Make sure you ask the parents where these magical training tools are located before she has to go.

② If you're at a public toilet, be sure to use a disposable toilet cover (or two) to give the little one a clean place to sit.

③ Unfasten the child's pants and underpants if she needs help.

④ Explain what you're doing as you go, so she can learn the necessary steps to do it herself. Remember, potty training is a learning experience and *you* are the teacher.

⑤ Help lift the child onto the toilet seat if she is too small to get on it by herself. She may also need to hang on to your arm for support. If the child can pee standing up, make sure you position him so he aims into the bowl and not anywhere else.

⑥ Wipe the child with toilet paper or baby wipes before refastening her clothes. (Always wipe girls from front to back.)

⑦ Have the child wash her hands with you. You can tell her she's done washing after she sings "Happy Birthday" twice. Then congratulate her for completing a successful potty training session.

Dealing with Accidents When They Happen

Despite your best efforts, kids will pee in their pants sometimes. It's not fun to deal with, but it's important to stay positive throughout the child's potty training days, even when he makes mistakes. Here's how you can deal with accidents like a pro.

① Always be prepared. Never leave the house without clean underwear or clean diapers, baby wipes, a fresh pair of clothes, and some plastic bags. Some parents may already have this stuff prepared in a shoulder bag.

② Even if an accident happens in public, don't make a big deal out of it. And don't make him feel bad. Instead, say, "Good try!"

③ Bring the child to the nearest bathroom or private area. Sometimes it helps to plan ahead for this—for example, only bring the child to restaurants and stores with large bathroom areas.

④ Remove any soiled clothes and put them in a plastic bag if you're in public, or the appropriate laundry receptacle if you're at home.

⑤ Wipe the kid down with baby wipes, and put fresh underwear, or a diaper, and clothes on him. Now all you have left to do is wash your hands!

TALES FROM THE CRIB

It's difficult to predict what will happen while you're babysitting. Whether it's an incident involving learning to share or fussiness over a meal—we must always expect the unexpected and prepare ourselves to control any situation that may occur.

One thing I was definitely not expecting was to find myself listening to four-year-old Lauren talk about her boyfriend, Jack. She smiled while recounting how they play on the monkey bars together and told me the story of when he asked her to marry him (they were going down the slide—how romantic!).

She looked at me, puzzled, as I was laughing along, and I realized how sure of her love she was. That's one of the best parts of babysitting, though—getting to know the kids you're with, and watching them over time as they mature and grow. I love sitting for kids who are young enough to believe in fairy tales and Santa Claus because they have active, developing imaginations not yet tainted by society. That definitely describes Lauren, and I just hope that I'm invited to the wedding!

—Audrey, 14

8. GETTING KIDS DRESSED

Making sure kids are properly clothed is an important part of a babysitter's to-do list. Babies need your help getting their arms and legs into onesies. Some two-year-olds just hate wearing shoes. Most kids can't even dress themselves without you until they're about four years old! And when kids start having opinions about clothes, you have a totally different experience.

Imagine you're babysitting for a very fashionable little kid, which is thrilling because you, too, are a stylista. When it's time to choose her outfit for the day, you furiously comb the drawers for the cutest stuff you can possibly find. Purple tights, yes! Green jumper, yes! Orange cowboy hat, obviously! By the end of this hour-long ordeal, she looks like a three-foot-tall kaleidoscope, and it's soooo cuuuute!!!

And then, buzzkill hits. It's Saturday. She has soccer practice. And it just rained all over the turf. Then you realize you have to leave in five minutes.

You beg. You plead. You fight. But this blinding rainbow child is just not getting into shin guards now.

So you should be prepared to help little ones change into everything from school clothes to pajamas to sports uniforms for muddy days. While there's no way to make dressing time go perfectly every day, there are things you can do to expedite the process, and crazy color dress-up time right before soccer practice probably isn't one of them!

① **Ask for instructions.** Kids have different wardrobe requirements depending on their age, their clothing preferences, and what their parents want them to wear. Parents know best. They even know better than the most stylish, opinionated kids, so be sure to ask your bosses what the deal is before you let the kids go nuts. Here are some questions you'll want to ask:

- *Can the child dress himself? What kind of help does he need?*

- *Where do you keep the socks, shoes, shirts, pants— (you get the idea)?*

- *Where do you put dirty clothes?*

- *Does he have to wear a school uniform?*

- *Does he require a sports uniform or any other equipment for scheduled activities?*

- *If the child is in a wheelchair (or has other special needs), are there any considerations I should take when I put clothes on or take them off?*

② **Plan ahead.** Rushing may agitate kids, increasing the risk of an outburst. Give yourself plenty of time to dress them. Factor in potential delays, like having to chase little ones around the house, or having to find their black shoes because they won't wear their brown ones. Also, plot smooth moves to save time, such as untying and loosening shoes *before* asking kids to put them on.

③ **Make it a joint effort.** Toddlers and older kids will like dressing more if you involve them in the process. For example, one-year-olds can probably remove their own socks, and preschoolers may want to pick their own shirt or pants. Just make sure they're being reasonable. Encouraging children to dress themselves will teach them to be more independent.

④ **Check for pitfalls.** Kids are clumsy enough as it is, so you don't want any clothing safety hazards on your hands. Before letting kids loose in their new outfits, check that their pants aren't too long and make sure their shoes are laced (or velcroed) nice and tight. Oh, and don't let them run around in their socks. That's a big slip just waiting to happen.

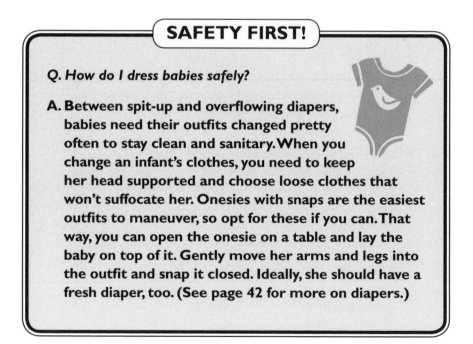

SAFETY FIRST!

Q. How do I dress babies safely?

A. Between spit-up and overflowing diapers, babies need their outfits changed pretty often to stay clean and sanitary. When you change an infant's clothes, you need to keep her head supported and choose loose clothes that won't suffocate her. Onesies with snaps are the easiest outfits to maneuver, so opt for these if you can. That way, you can open the onesie on a table and lay the baby on top of it. Gently move her arms and legs into the outfit and snap it closed. Ideally, she should have a fresh diaper, too. (See page 42 for more on diapers.)

9. PLAYTIME

So you're relatively new at a babysitting gig, and you want to make a fun first impression. You buy Barbies to surprise the twin girls before bedtime. After all, Barbies were totally your thing when you were their age. They're going to *love* them.

But when you open those glorious, nostalgic pink boxes, the kids couldn't care less about the blonde hair and teeny stethoscopes. Instead, the little brats run to the den and invent a game of their own—one that involves a giant pillow fort that Godzilla (you) must destroy at all costs.

Why Godzilla, of all things? you think. *These Barbies can totally check your blood pressure and read it back to you! And how do these kids know about 1950s Japanese horror flicks anyway?*

Face it, sitter: Blood-Pressure Barbie is no more.

Kids' playtime preferences can be totally unpredictable. Nobody holds the secret to pleasing every kid right off the bat (and no, snack bribes don't count). So instead of sticking to a premeditated plan, let things happen as they will. There's nothing wrong with Barbies, but these kids just aren't into them. Move on. Embrace your new Godzilla identity. And be creative with it: Godzilla could have a British accent or wear a shoe on her head. The possibilities are endless.

Structuring Play by Age

Every kid is different. If you had to tattoo one babysitting rule on your forehead, it would be just that. But even so, kids in certain age groups have certain preferences. You wouldn't give an eight-year-old a baby rattle or feed pizza to a newborn, right? Taking kids' ages into consideration will make life a lot easier for them and for you. Here are the general age groups and what each one is into.

Age 0 to 12 months

When it comes to babies, there's not much of a difference between playtime and any other time of day (like bedtime or snack time, for instance). Playtime never really ends for them, and everything's a kind of game. And even though babies don't exactly do much, there are lots of ways to play with them. They get a kick out of cool sounds, soft touches, simulated Superman lifts, playing peek-a-boo, and just watching you mess around with things like funny puppets and small blinky lights. And even though you might think that nose-nuzzling is boring, most babies love it.

Toddlers

Toddlers are more active participants than babies. They like to play alongside other toddlers, but they're not quite sharing or fully interacting with other kids yet. They do like to lug around toys and stuffed animals. They also like to show off their newly acquired skills, like kicking. Unfortunately, they don't know how clumsy they are. So you need to keep an eye on them and put a stop to any potentially dangerous stunts.

Luckily, toddlers are all about imitation, so you're more in control than you think. Keep them busy with role-playing games, like pretend cooking, train conducting, or dress up. Or spend the afternoon organizing toy cars into categories like big, little, red, and blue. (They can usually recognize patterns, like colors, numbers, or size at this age.) If all else fails, read aloud. Books are very visually stimulating for kids, especially the ones with surprise pop-ups or textile elements. Kids at this age also love pushing sound buttons on books that play funny noises. But, toddlers may try to manhandle the pages, so don't expect to finish the book.

Preschoolers

These are those magical ages between toddler toys and video games when kids love using their imagination. You'll score some points by serving make-believe meals to a group of dolls, helping kids build a fort for their toys, or initiating a game of hide-and-seek while wearing superhero costumes (suggestion: raid the towel closet for some home-grown capes!). And they're also into physical activities, like riding tricycles, running, and climbing. They probably can't read yet, but they're more engaged in books. So interactive books, like ones that come with stickers, are fair game. Preschoolers are fun because they are so active. But, be sure to keep an eye on them at all times—you never know when one will try to run into the street, climb up on the counter, or dip her hands in a dangerous cleaning liquid.

Be warned. Even if playtime is going smoothly, preschoolers may get randomly rigid and say no or throw fits when you try a new tactic. Yes, it's annoying. And no, it doesn't make any sense why the kid loves patrol cars but hates helicopters all of a sudden (it was totally the other way around five seconds ago). But why waste time arguing about law enforcement vehicles? Instead, relax. Ditch the helicopters, and don't be afraid to step out of the game and ask what the kid wants.

While preschoolers like to play with other kids their age, some fighting and tantrums are inevitable. You should orchestrate fun, fair, physical games with very simple rules (think musical chairs, duck duck goose, or pin the tail on the donkey). If you're the almighty dictator of the rules, this could minimize fighting between the children. (Read more about fighting and discipline on page 56.)

Kids 5 and up

Older kids are typically comfortable with structured play, like sports, video games, and board games. Sometimes they're a little *too comfy* rotting their brains in front of the TV. But if you can manage to get them off the couch, educational games like Scrabble and creative activities like birdhouse building or other arts and crafts are ways to prove to them that the world won't end if they drop the game controller. Eventually, kids outgrow playtime, so don't take it personally if they snub you. The older kids get, the more important their friends are. Did you want to hang out with your sitter all day when you were twelve? Lame!

TALES FROM THE CRIB

When I first started babysitting (around age fourteen), I went in thinking it was going to be a breeze. I was a teenager, they were little kids; clearly I had authority. But if there's one thing I've learned after years of babysitting, it's to not underestimate the children. For many kids, the parents leaving a babysitter in charge for a night is like when there's a substitute teacher in school. As any high school and even middle school student will tell you, a sub means no assigned seats, no homework, and basically freedom to do whatever you want. Even though they're young, kids feel the same way about a babysitter.

It was only after a few weeks when the kids started asking about watching TV—which was against the family "no TV" rule. Annie, who rarely finished her vegetables when I made dinner, would pull something like, "If I finish these carrots, can I pretty, pretty please watch TV?" I knew, technically, the rule, but I also knew that if Annie finished her vegetables her mom would be very impressed. Once the kids realized I was hesitating before saying no, they'd come in for the kill. "Yeah, please!" Trevor whined. "I finished all of my homework! And Mom and Dad have been letting us watch TV on week nights sometimes." This, I doubted was true. But watching TV was going to make them happy and the things they'd do in order to get me to say yes would make the parents happy, so it was a win-win. These were two young kids who had managed to take full advantage of the lack of parents and convince me to bend the rules. Like I said ... don't underestimate them.

—Cheyenne, 18

In the end, playtime is supposed to be *fun*. Your ultimate goal shouldn't be to "wow" the kids, or be a stickler about game rules. Rather, it's an opportunity for you to relax and form a comfortable bond with the children while keeping them safe. Once you've got playtime down, both you and the kids will look forward to your visits, and you'll have a whole litany of awesome games and inside jokes to choose from.

10. USING CONSTRUCTIVE DISCIPLINE

You're on the afterschool shift, and everything is going great. The kid behaved on the walk home from school. She ate like a champ. And now she's in the corner, making a nice little drawing of a cat... on the wall.

Quickly, you spring into action, fueled by the fear that your bosses (her parents) will skin you alive. You grab the crayons out of her hand. She flies into a rage. She yells at you. She screams. She cries. She even starts stomping around, throwing things. Everything is officially out of control.

Let's just say, that didn't go well.

Discipline Basics

It can be maddening, and even heartbreaking when a child disobeys you. If a child doesn't want to do her homework, if she's yelling and screaming in the middle of a grocery store, if she's late coming home, or if she's writing on the walls, it's very easy to feel really stressed, and even personally slighted. But getting really mad, or beating yourself up over a child's outburst isn't going to help. When a child is disobeying you, discipline is your best friend. Discipline isn't always punishment, and it's certainly not screaming and yelling. More often, discipline is about patience, listening, constructive feedback, and sometimes, even ignoring a problem until it dies. In the case above, you'd be right to intervene if you catch the kid writing on the wall. She's breaking the rules! But once she starts throwing that tantrum, it's time to back off and let her lose steam.

To help get through these trying times, here are the discipline basics.

① **Get the routine down.** Discipline problems often happen when there's a rupture in the child's daily routine. Maybe you ate dinner a little later than usual. Maybe the kid didn't get enough sleep. Sometimes, certain objects or situations will send a kid into a fit. You should get to know the child, avoid his triggers, and stick to the schedule as best as you can.

② **Ask the parents.** The parents are your best resource for discipline issues. Before they leave you in charge, ask them about any discipline issues, and what kinds of tactics they use to ensure good behavior.

③ **Distract.** The "Look over there!" approach isn't foolproof, but it's worth a shot. If you feel a tantrum coming, try distracting the kid with something fun. Do a crazy dance, show her a new toy, or play with her hair. It may just stop the kid dead in her tracks before she engages in a scream-fest.

④ **Ignore.** Even though it's impossible to ignore a loud tantrum or whiny spell, it helps if you pretend it's not even happening. The kid should eventually realize that her fits won't get her any attention. After she calms down, you can explain nicely that tantrums won't get her what she wants.

⑤ **Call a time out.** If the child is hitting you, throwing things, or causing major terror, you may want to enforce a time out. To do this, you'd usually tell the kid to sit somewhere boring in the house for a few minutes (try one minute per year of the child's age). This tells the kid plainly that she's done something wrong, while also giving her an opportunity to chill out. Don't use time outs unless the parents specifically tell you to, however. Time outs are just one tactic, and not all parents use them.

⑥ **Call the parents.** If you've exhausted all other options, you can call Mom and Dad for advice. However, you should only use this tactic as a last resort. After all, they hired you to handle things yourself. Sometimes, threatening to call the parents is enough to snap the kids into good behavior. But repeated threats without any follow-through may lessen the effect of this disciplinary approach.

Disciplining Two (or More) Kids

Dealing with siblings or playdates is a whole different ball game than dealing with an only child. While you can still use one or more of constructive discipline tactics (see page 56), getting the job done can get more complicated as jealousy, bullying, excluding, and fighting rear their ugly heads during playtime, or over dinner. Below are some do's and don'ts when dealing with multiple misbehaving children.

① **Do encourage friendly play.** If a fight breaks out, you should try and mediate through fair negotiation. If the children are fighting over a toy, for example, you should encourage them to share it. If you play a game with  a couple of competitive siblings or playdates, have them work together instead of against each other. For example, you can play a board game and put them on the same team against you.

② **Don't pick favorites.** Whether you want to or not, you'll probably choose a favorite child who you would rather spend your time with, especially if one sibling is really well-behaved and the other sibling is a complete nightmare. However, you should never, ever show it. Never compare children out loud. Don't give imbalanced consequences. Always make sure you're paying equal attention to both children. You don't want to rouse jealousy and anger, or fighting might erupt.

③ **Do keep kids entertained.** A fight can ensue if the children are tired, hungry, or bored. Don't plan strenuous activities around bedtime or before meal time, and try to keep both kids entertained. If the younger siblings or playdates are relentlessly annoying the older kids, you should try entertaining the little guys yourself.

④ **Don't tolerate teasing.** Teasing can be very painful, whether it's between siblings or play dates. It's important to intervene when you see signs of teasing and make sure the children feel protected.

⑤ **Do separate kids who can't play nice.** If the children are constantly fighting, or if the fighting becomes violent, break them up. It'll distract them from their anger and defuse the situation. Let them know that whoever hits will face consequences. Live up to your promise with time outs, revoked privileges, or a call to the parents as soon as any violence flares up.

SAFETY FIRST!

Q: *What are the signs of child abuse?*

A: Any kind of child abuse is when a child is verbally berated, beaten excessively, or sexually molested. Some signs of abuse are when the victim:

- **has unexplained bruises, cuts, broken bones, or other injuries or expresses inappropriate sexual knowledge or behavior;**

- **seems depressed, withdrawn, or excessively angry;**

- **has serious difficulty sleeping.**

Remember, some of these symptoms (like bruises and cuts) may just be a natural result of being an active little kid, but if you suspect that a child has been abused, immediately talk to a trusted adult.

11. HELPING WITH HOMEWORK

After endless prodding, you finally got the eight-year-old to do his homework—but he's very obviously not happy about it. He's fiddling with the worksheets, biding time, and hemming and hawing over how hard it is.

Luckily, it's English—your best subject! Immediately you sit down to help. You correct his mistakes (there are a *lot* of them) and breeze through the work. It's all coming back to you. You're a pronoun, capitalization, apostrophe-making machine! Suddenly, the kid leaves to go to the bathroom. Ten minutes later, you hear the TV blaring. The worst part is, you look at the worksheet and realize in horror that you did the whole thing yourself.

You don't have to be a world-class tutor to be a babysitter. If the parents want a professional teacher to help kids with their homework, they should hire one. However, babysitters should be able to offer children *some* assistance with school assignments and projects, even if this means simply convincing them to do their homework in the first place. This isn't always easy, since anything is more fun than homework, and it's even harder to do if the child feels challenged by it. Here's how to encourage kids to get the job done, and how to avoid feeling like a sucker who does all the work.

Stick to the Schedule. Ask the parents about the children's homework schedule, and stick to it. You may want to give them a ten-minute warning before homework time to avoid resistance. Also keep in mind that kids will be terrible little workers if you force study time when they're tired or hungry, so aim to have homework time after they've eaten, and way before bedtime.

Take away distractions. This basically means no TV, iPods, cell phones, or noisy siblings should be allowed in the room so the kid can really concentrate. And if he needs to use a computer to get his homework done, make sure all chat windows are closed. He won't accomplish anything if he's too busy answering instant messages!

Create a fun study environment. Small children are more likely to do their homework if you make it fun. Clear off a table, put colorful pencils and school supplies all around. This will provide fun associations with school work.

Stick around to help. Some homework comes with instructions for parents and caregivers. So find out if you're supposed to get involved. Even if you're not, be available for questions. If you're babysitting for young children, look over their homework when they're done. If you're dealing with older kids, be honest if something is too hard for you. A lot of grown-ups don't remember how to do long division, so don't beat yourself up if you don't know the answer. Instead, help them find someone who does.

Don't answer for them. Even if a child is struggling with his homework, you shouldn't answer the questions for him or he'll never learn to do it himself. Guide the child to the right answer and make sure he understands how he got there.

12. BATHING CHILDREN SAFELY

You've been playing in the mud with a three-year-old, and while it was probably the best time you've ever had in a dirt pile, the little girl is now in desperate need of a bath.

But when you start to fill up the tub, you discover that she, the same girl who was so unafraid to play with giant bugs a few minutes ago, is petrified of the bath drain. She's convinced that it will suck her into a terrifying netherworld filled with child-eating drain monsters. So when you suggest a bath, she throws a tantrum and sullies up the couch with her muddy pants. She couldn't care less about the stains because, to her, you're a mean, mean babysitter.

Kids can get pretty dirty, and they may need your help getting clean—whether they want it or not. Some parents want their babysitter to take care of the bathing ritual. Others prefer to take care of it themselves. (You can always use a warm washcloth as an alternative to a bath.) If your bosses haven't specified what they want you to do, ask them. You may even need a demo. Bathing babies, for example, can be a little tricky for beginners, and you probably shouldn't do it unless you've gotten a few hands-on tutorials from the parents. Also ask if parents want siblings to bathe together or separately. This could lead to more questions, like who's going to watch the kid who's not in the tub?

Ultimately, bath time can be a scary time for kids, so you need a plan to keep things fun and disaster-free—and safe from drain beasts. Here are some tips.

Keep water levels low. Little kids can easily drown in a tub, so never fill it all the way. The water should only be two to three inches high for babies, and for older children, the water should come to their waists when they sit down.

Test the temperature. Before putting a kid in the tub, you should make sure the temperature is comfortably warm. You don't want to burn or freeze him to tears! Test the temperature of the water by wetting the palm side of your wrist, or use your elbow. These spots are more sensitive than your fingers.

Don't push, just help. Tubs are slippery, especially for clumsy little kids. Hold their hands as they climb in and out of the tub. And don't let go until they're sitting in a stable position. If a child is nervous about getting in the tub, don't force him in. Some little kids are still learning what baths are all about. So be gentle, and don't criticize their fears, even if drain monsters are the funniest things you've ever heard of.

Make it fun. If a kid is reluctant to get in the tub, offer to bring some waterproof, safe toys into the tub. Or promise to read her her favorite book or sing her favorite song while she takes a bath. Whatever it takes. Even if she is beyond clean or after she gets clean, you should let her play in the tub for a little while. It'll make bath time something to look forward to in the future.

Wash their hair. (Optional.) Children don't need their hair washed every day, so ask the parents about this beforehand. If the answer is yes, you mainly want to avoid getting water or specially labeled "no tears" shampoo in kids' eyes. Tilt their heads back, and use a plastic cup or bowl to pour water on their hair. Guard their eyes by placing your other hand lightly on their forehead. Lather the specified shampoo in their hair and rinse it off (again use the cup and keep their heads tilted back).

Supervise, supervise, supervise! You've gotten them in the tub, you've washed their hair, you've read them three books. You're a bath-time gold medalist! But that doesn't mean your job is done. Stay in the room to make sure the kids sit relatively still. Also make sure they don't bonk their heads on the faucet, and most important, make sure they keep their heads above the water. Even leaving the room for a minute to answer the phone or the doorbell can lead to a potential drowning. If you absolutely have to leave the room, wrap up the child in a towel and bring her with you.

Prep for the post-tub procedure. Before you gently coax the kids out of the bath, have a clean towel handy, as well as their next outfits. When they're out of the tub, dry their bodies and hair gently with the towel. Some parents will ask you to use rash cream or moisturizer for dry skin. Afterward, dress the kids (see page 48 for tips). If the children have long, tangly hair, run a comb through it while it's still wet. You can spray or rub leave-in conditioner into their hair before you start brushing to help minimize shrieking.

Bathe in case of emergency. There will be times when a bath wasn't part of the parents' instructions, but the kid really, really needs one. If that happens on your watch, call the parents to explain the situation. And ask them if they have any specific instructions. Below are some examples of bathing emergencies.

- *The children have urinated or soiled themselves, and they're not wearing diapers (or the diapers didn't do the job).*

- *The children are extremely filthy or sticky. If the kids have been playing outside, they may fall into this category.*

- *You suspect lice, scabies, fleas, or another infestation that could put their health (and yours) at risk.*

SAFETY FIRST!

Q. *What do I do if a kid begins to drown?*

A. First of all, it's important to become **CPR** certified before accepting any babysitting job. Hopefully this is a skill you'll never have to use, but if you're caught in a situation where a child is drowning, remove the child from the water. Ask if he's alright and try to rouse him. If he's unconscious, not breathing, or if he has no pulse, call 911 immediately. Then you will have to administer **CPR** (cardiopulmonary resuscitation). If anyone is around to help, instruct someone to call 911 immediately, and then begin **CPR**. If you're alone or if you're not already trained in **CPR**, here's what you can do:

If you are ever in doubt about what to do, or how to do it, always call 911 at any time.

1. Place the child on her back on a hard surface.

2. For children ages one through eight, place the heel of your hand on the child's chest, right between the child's nipples. For a younger child, place just two of your fingers in the same spot.

3. Push down, using your body weight. You want to push down at least two inches each time for children ages one through eight, and for babies, you'll want to push just 1.5 inches. Push one hundred times per minute.

4. Do these compressions for two minutes before calling 911.*

*Instructions taken from the American Heart Association 2005 American Heart Association guidelines for cardiopulmonary resuscitation and emergency cardiovascular care: Part 3: Overview of CPR.

13. PUTTING KIDS TO BED

It's your favorite time of day: the kid's bedtime. Soon, you'll have a few hours of precious peace before the parents come home. You'll finally be able to text back the friend who's been trying to reach you. You'll finally check the score of the big game. You'll finally sit down.

Not surprisingly, the kid is not looking forward to bedtime as much as you are. Sensing that it's time for bed, he just came up with a laundry list of activities to do. He broke out the video games, the board games, even the homework that he was so unwilling to do a few minutes ago. He's clearly wound up and exhausted, but when you say it's time for bed, he screams no and starts to cry. By now, you're so tired yourself, you don't want to put up a fight. You reason, *maybe if I indulge him and play with him some more, he'll tire himself out!*

But before you know it, two hours have gone by. The parents are pulling up in the driveway, and the kid, now delirious from lack of sleep, is trying to parachute down the stairs with a garbage bag. Enjoy explaining your way out of this one.

Kids can be very fussy about getting their Zs. While it's almost impossible to get children totally psyched for bedtime, there are ways to make it go a lot smoother than that scenario.

Learn the routine. Children will go down easier if bedtime happens according to their regular schedule. As always, your biggest source of information is the parents. Some questions to ask Mom and Dad include:

- *What time does the child go to bed?*

- *Does he need a nap? If so, how often and how long does he sleep?*

- *What's her usual bedtime ritual? Does she brush her teeth by herself? Does she wear special pajamas? Does she need a story, lullaby, nightlight, or all of the above?*

- *Does she need you to stay with her until she falls asleep, or is she OK alone?*

- *Does he have nightmares? If so, what's the best way to put him back to sleep?*

Issue a ten-minute warning. Let children know they have ten minutes to wrap up any games or activities before they start getting ready for bed. Most kids need some time to get adjusted to the idea of bedtime, and a sudden command will force them to react impulsively. Either way, they may put up a fight. If they do, turn to page 56 for some advice.

Keep it quiet. If you want to encourage sleep, don't blast the TV or chat loudly on the phone. The noise will not only wake up the children, but they'll also want to climb out of bed because they want to watch TV, too! Also, if you're babysitting small children, keeping noise levels down allows you to hear them cry.

Give parents an update. Let parents know if you notice any sleep issues. Maybe the toddler seemed fussy and was constantly rubbing his eyes long before his scheduled nap time. Or maybe he was waking up often and having a hard time falling back asleep. The parents may decide to change the routine based on what you tell them.

SAFETY FIRST!

Q. Is it true that babies can die from sleeping?

A. As shocking as it may sound, even sleeping can be dangerous for babies. Sudden infant death syndrome (SIDS) is when a baby under one year old, dies suddenly while sleeping, without any explanation—meaning that doctors can't determine what caused the death. The reason you should care: About one in five SIDS cases happen while an infant is being cared for by someone other than a parent. No one knows what causes SIDS, but there are ways to promote a safe sleep. For instance, babies who sleep on their stomachs are three times more likely to die of SIDS. So, when putting infants to sleep, make sure to:

– Place them on their backs. Even if they're on their sides, they may roll on their stomachs and risk SIDS.

– Remove surrounding toys, clothes, rags, or anything that could suffocate them.

– Choose sleepwear with covered feet or special sleep bags instead of blankets, which can easily smother them.

14. KEEPING KIDS HEALTHY

You're babysitting for a four-year-old socialite. You've never seen anyone with so many freaking playdates. One day you have to take her to the zoo with her best friend. The next, it's a pool party. The next, it's a giant sleepover. She's got so many engagements, she deserves her own reality show.

Unfortunately, this is the same girl who hates to take baths. She also hates medicine, hand soap, rest, and vitamin C. You've been lax on all these things when you care for her. One day, she comes home from a playdate with a not-so-surprising stomach bug. Fever, vomiting, diarrhea—she's got it all. And you're left to clean up the mess.

When it comes to kids, accidents happen. So does mucus, vomit, little-kid germs, and diarrhea. They also often get cuts and scrapes. They may have asthma, colic, or allergies. And all of these things can flair up on your watch. When they do, it's important to know how to handle it. While you should call 911 when major disasters strike, like broken bones or anything that involves a lot of blood, it helps to know how to deal with minor emergencies. Here are some common medical problems that babysitters face while on the job, along with tips on how to solve them.

Allergies

Some children get bad reactions from things like shellfish, soy, nuts, dust, pet dander, and pollen. Symptoms can range from itchiness and rashes to vomiting and life-threatening shock.

SNEEZE
EASE

What to Do

✔ Prevent potential allergic reactions by asking parents what the triggers are, and keeping the kids away from anything that could set off an attack.

✔ Get the 411 on any medication. Parents may ask you to give the child over-the-counter or prescription allergy medicine. Kids with more serious allergies may even need regular shots. If there is a risk of a child going into anaphylactic shock (see below), his parents should outline the emergency protocol. If you're panicked, call 911 immediately and follow the instructions.

✔ Get certified to inject a shot or administer CPR. If you are not qualified, don't try it. You might do more harm than good.

When to Worry

✔ If a child is lightheaded, nauseous, short of breath, unconscious, breaking out in a rash, or vomiting, he may be going into anaphylactic shock. This can eventually cause a child to stop breathing, and may even stop his heartbeat. Call 911 immediately if this happens, even if you are trained to administer the epinephrine shot or CPR.

Asthma

Asthma is a disease that causes inflammation of the airways. The parents will usually let you know if their child is asthmatic. If he is, make sure you get specific instructions about how to deal with it. During an attack, a child's respiratory system swells up and blocks air from flowing freely. An asthma attack can be pretty scary. The child may cough or wheeze excessively, and in serious cases, he may not be able to breathe at all. An asthma attack can be triggered by exercise, irritating fumes, or from allergies, so it's important to stay away from anything that can set one off.

What to Do

✔ Ask parents for a complete rundown of asthma meds as well as the details for their emergency action plan.

✔ Set reminders for yourself if you need to juggle a number of medications.

✔ Carry the child's inhaler—a pocketsize device that squirts asthma medicine into the child's mouth—on you at all times. Some kids may need to use fast-acting inhalers when they're about to exercise, or when they feel an attack coming on.

✔ Have the child's parents show you how to use any additional asthma equipment that may be needed. Children around toddler age and younger can't use inhalers because the dosage is too unpredictable. You may have to apply a facemask that attaches to a machine called a nebulizer. It sounds scary, but it's a pretty simple device.

When to Worry

✔ If a child is having difficulty breathing, even if he has not been diagnosed with asthma, call 911 immediately.

✔ If, despite treatment (for instance the child has used his inhaler), the child with asthma is still having a severe reaction—which can include widening nostrils, straining her abdominal muscles, and stopping in the middle of a sentence to catch her breath—always call 911, even if you are unsure if the attack is serious. Better safe than sorry.

Colic

When an otherwise healthy, well-fed baby cries nonstop for no reason, the baby may have colic. Colic is one of the great, irritating mysteries of medicine. Nobody really knows what causes it, and the only known symptoms are a healthy baby who cries for more than three hours a day, three days a week or more, for more than three weeks. The baby's crying jags generally happen around the same time every day and can be accompanied by screaming and fist clenching. There is no cure, but it usually goes away on its own when the child is about three months old.

What to Do

✔ Try all the things you'd normally try for any crying baby, like giving her a pacifier, rocking, feeding, singing, or even leaving her alone in her crib for a minute.

✔ Exercise your kindest patience and try to not get overwhelmed. Colicky babies will often keep crying, so you'll need to keep calm and not get too frustrated.

When to Worry

✔ If a baby cries longer than three hours, call the parents to see if they have any solutions. A colicky baby can make it sound like the skies are falling, but the condition is not actually dangerous. Episodes usually last up to three hours.

✔ If you suspect that she's injured or ill, call the parents and 911 if necessary. Also, let the parents know if the baby is refusing to eat or sleep due to incessant crying.

Cuts and Scrapes

Since the dawn of time, children have been getting cuts and scrapes while playing sports, falling downstairs, or even just walking around the house. These are slight skin injuries, and they sometimes result in bleeding.

What to Do

✔ Hold a clean bandage or cloth on a bloody wound for about ten to twenty minutes, or until the blood stops flowing.

✔ Clean it with a damp sterile cotton pad or antiseptic wipe. (Make sure to get all the nasty dirt out so the cut doesn't get infected.)

✔ Apply an antibiotic cream, like Neosporin, to keep bad bacteria away.

✔ Cover the wound with a colorful bandage. (Kitties and dinosaurs are always safe bets.)

When to Worry

✔ If the cut doesn't stop bleeding after step one, or if a considerable amount of dirt or junk stays lodged in the wound, you should call the 911 and follow their instructions.

✔ If the wound is bigger or deeper than a minor scrape—you may need to call 911 so the child can get stitches.

✔ If the child has trouble moving the wounded limb, you should call 911. She may have sprained or fractured something.

✔ If the child cuts himself on rusty metal, he may have to get a tetanus shot—or if he's bitten by an animal that may have rabies, he may need treatment. If this happens on your watch, call 911.

Call the parents or seek medical help if any of the symptoms above are present.

SAFETY FIRST!

Q: *What do I do if a child ingests toxic materials?*

A: **Unfortunately, it happens all the time. Children mistake cough medicine for juice, or house cleaning products for toothpaste. These mistakes can lead to serious illness, or even death. If you do see a child ingest a toxic chemical, call 911 and also 1-800-222-1222, which will link you to your nearest Poison Control Center in the US. Have some information on hand, like the child's age, how long ago he swallowed or ingested the poison, and what kind of toxic material it is. In the meantime, make sure you always read the label, and that all poisonous materials are out of the child's reach.**

Diarrhea

You probably already know what diarrhea is—runny or watery bowel movements—and if the child you're babysitting is complaining of stomach pains and constantly going to the bathroom, he probably has it. It can be caused by anything from food poisoning to a stomach virus. And a bad case of the runs can lead to dehydration, especially in babies.

What to Do

✔ Avoid diarrhea in the first place by washing your hands (and the child's hands) often, especially before touching food and after using the bathroom, coughing, sneezing, or handling pets.

✔ Wash food thoroughly before serving it, and don't serve anything that could potentially lead to an upset stomach. For example, if a child is lactose intolerant, don't serve him dairy. Or if food has been sitting out for a while, throw it away; don't feed it to the kid.

✔ Call the child's parents for advice on administering any diarrhea medication. They might have home remedies they'd like to you try first and sometimes all a child needs is time.

✔ Consult the parents about the fluids you should give a child with diarrhea. Continue to give breast milk or formula to babies to keep them hydrated. For toddlers, see if there are any oral rehydration drinks, such as Pedialyte, in the house to help replace lost nutrients. Have older children drink oral rehydration drinks, too. Often plain water, soda, sports drinks, and fruit juices can make diarrhea worse because they don't have the right sugars and salts to help rehydrate a child.

When to Worry

✔ If the child is vomiting.

✔ If he refuses to drink liquids.

✔ If he has a fever above 102°F.

✔ If his stomach aches are extremely painful, or if there's blood or mucus in his diarrhea (yes, you have to look at it).

✔ If the diarrhea doesn't go away after a couple of days.

Call the parents or seek medical help if any of the symptoms above are present.

Fever

If a child's temperature is running higher than normal (98.6°F),
then he probably has a fever. Usually, this means that his body is heating up from fighting off an infection. Fevers in teens and adults aren't typically dangerous, but for young children and babies, a fever can indicate a serious infection. Sometimes a fever even indicates a major illness, like pneumonia or meningitis when coupled with additional symptoms.

What to Do

✔ If the child's forehead is warm to the touch and she complains about not feeling well, take her temperature. If it's high, let the parents know about the abnormal temperature change. Low-grade fevers will often go away on their own, without treatment, but it's still important to let parents know.

✔ Administer a fever-reducing medicine like Children's Tylenol or Children's Advil if the parents ask you to.

✔ Make sure the child has plenty of hydrating liquids like Pedialyte.

When to Worry

✔ If the child is younger than three months and has a temperature higher than 100.4°F.

✔ If the child is older than three months and he has a temperature up to 102°F and seems uncomfortable or overly fatigued, or if he have a temperature over 102°F and it doesn't drop after a day.

✔ If the child is vomiting and refusing to eat or drink.

✔ If the child has a fever after being left in a hot car or if the fever is accompanied by seizures, call 911 immediately.

Call the parents or seek medical help if any of the symptoms above are present.

SAFETY FIRST!

Q. How do I take a child's temperature safely?

A. If you need to take a child's temperature, ask the parents how they want it done: through the child's ear, through her armpit, or in her mouth. Whatever the procedure, always clean thermometers before and after use with rubbing alcohol or soap or tepid water. And don't leave a child alone if she has a thermometer inside of her. She could choke or suffer internal damage.

Nosebleeds

If a kid picks her nose, or worse, if she picks her nose in a dry environment, she may get a nasty nosebleed. A nosebleed is usually when blood gushes out of somebody's septum, the chamber that separates the nostrils. They're messy, but they're rarely dangerous.

What to Do

✔ Sit the child upright and have her lean forward. Pinch the child's nose, or have the child pinch her own nose shut to put pressure on the bleeding point and help stop the blood flow. Have her breathe through her mouth for about ten minutes. If the bleeding hasn't stopped by then, have the child (lightly) blow her nose, pinch it, and repeat. Most important, don't let the kid pick her nose again no matter how badly she wants to.

When To Worry

✔ If the child's nose bleeds for more than twenty minutes.

✔ If you think his nose is broken, or if he has persistent nosebleeds throughout the day.

Call the parents or seek medical help if any of the symptoms above are present.

15. AVOIDING PREVENTABLE EMERGENCIES

Your worst nightmare just started in the parents' kitchen: a fire. You're not sure how it happened, but if you had to hazard a guess—it probably had something to do with little Johnny pouring lighter fluid into the oven. Whoops—he wasn't blowing bubbles after all.

The fire starts out small, so you tell Johnny to leave the room while you try to wrangle the situation yourself. After all, you've seen movies with fires in them. So, you pour water on it, but that only seems to make the fire angrier. You blow on it, which spreads it to the refrigerator door, melting Johnny's beautiful macaroni art. Now panicked, you get the parents' fire extinguisher, only to realize you have no clue how to operate the thing.

By the time you and Johnny run out of the house and call the fire department, half of the kitchen has been consumed by flames, including the parents' phone numbers on the counter.

What should you do differently next time? Pretty much everything!

You read up on how to solve common problems and have all your emergency contacts on hand. But there are some things you can do (and not do) to avoid accidents and illnesses in the first place.

Do watch kids closely. You'll be amazed at how easily little kids hurt themselves. This is one reason why you should pay attention to them at all times. Save personal phone calls, text messages, and IMs for when the kids are fast asleep. And even if your favorite show is on, don't leave kids to play alone. You should never assume that they're totally safe from injury.

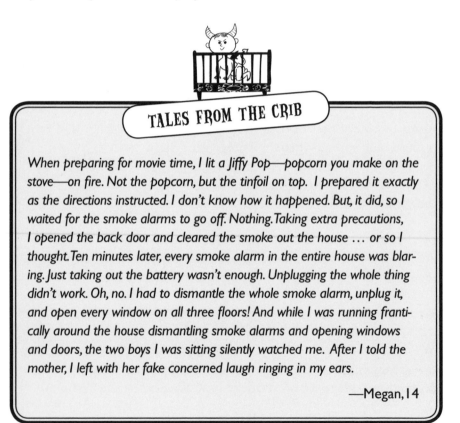

TALES FROM THE CRIB

When preparing for movie time, I lit a Jiffy Pop—popcorn you make on the stove—on fire. Not the popcorn, but the tinfoil on top. I prepared it exactly as the directions instructed. I don't know how it happened. But, it did, so I waited for the smoke alarms to go off. Nothing. Taking extra precautions, I opened the back door and cleared the smoke out the house ... or so I thought. Ten minutes later, every smoke alarm in the entire house was blaring. Just taking out the battery wasn't enough. Unplugging the whole thing didn't work. Oh, no. I had to dismantle the whole smoke alarm, unplug it, and open every window on all three floors! And while I was running frantically around the house dismantling smoke alarms and opening windows and doors, the two boys I was sitting silently watched me. After I told the mother, I left with her fake concerned laugh ringing in my ears.

—Megan, 14

Don't come to work sick. Children are particularly susceptible to germs that cause illnesses, like colds or flus. If the kids get sick, they could easily spread their germs to their siblings or classmates. If you're feeling ill, take time off.

Do ask for help. Nobody knows how to deal with every single problem. If you don't know how to handle a safety issue, don't guess. If Johnny gets an injury and you're not sure whether to wrap it in bandages or pump him full of antibiotics, you should always feel comfortable calling his parents, trusted adults, or medical professionals. You might even consider consulting your own parents.

Do say no to dangerous situations. This may seem obvious, but there's just no other way to put it. At some point, children will want to play with the stove, run with scissors, or light something on fire. They might even try to convince you that their parents let them do it all the time. Always trust your gut instinct and say no if something seems dangerous. If it's already too late and damage has been done, tell the parents what happened (even if you may have used poor judgment). Parents need to know what their kids have been up to, especially if they've been injured.

Don't panic. Even if you're stressed beyond belief in an emergency situation, try to remain in control. You're still the authority figure, and you don't want to scare the kids any further. Panicking will also impede your ability to make good decisions.

Emergency Call Sheet

Sure, everyone says not to panic during an emergency. But it's hard not to freak out if something really bad is going down. This is why you should have phone numbers for the parents, the police, the fire department, and a neighbor, and an extra emergency contact in an easy-to-find place so you're not frantically searching for the numbers later on. You can photocopy the sheet below and fill in important numbers for all your clients, or enter these numbers into your cell phone for each client.

Who to Call in Case of an Emergency

Police _____

Fire Department _____

Mom _____

Dad _____

Neighbor_____

Pediatrician _____

Poison Control Center _____

TALES FROM THE CRIB

This situation is what every babysitter dreads—when the first news that you have to deliver to the parents is that their child has a huge lump on her head ... and it's your fault. A few evenings ago I was babysitting two little girls, Sasha and Ava. Ava is five and Sasha is seven. After a dinner of bean-and-cheese burritos at our favorite local taqueria, the girls suggested we play with their new softball batting machine. I agreed, and went first to get a feel for the contraption. I took a few practice swings, and on the third swing I finally hit the end of the rod—and something else... Sasha's head! She immediately fell to the ground and let out a screaming cry. I ran to her and saw the lump on her head beginning to form already! I apologized over and over again, and Ava happily pretended to be the big sister for the night, running to get Sasha's favorite stuffed animal friends. I carried Sasha into the house, got an ice pack, and put her on the couch. Sasha was a great sport about the whole thing—when she heard she had to put ice on it, she decided that she would have an ice pack on her head literally the entire rest of the night. Even after I put her to bed she would come out when her ice got warm and get a new pack. When her parents got home and I had to break the news, they weren't too upset. They said it would teach her to not stand so close to the batting machine. I claimed responsibility, but they still didn't blame me. Surprisingly, I think how I handled the situation and how I continued to ask how Sasha was doing helped my reputation as a babysitter. Moral of the story: Don't hit a kid in the head with a bat, but if you do, you can still score babysitting points by handling the situation calmly and responsibly!

—Althea, 16

16. TAKING CARE OF YOURSELF

You've officially had it. Jane won't go to bed, Richie's nose won't stop bleeding, and Sean won't stop crying. You can hardly breathe, you're so frustrated. You feel a panic attack coming on. You feel faint. You feel hoarse. You're sure you feel a cold coming on. You resolve never to babysit for the rest of your life . . . starting immediately.

In protest, you sit on the couch and do nothing for hours. It feels great. But when you've finally calmed down, you realize that everything had gotten so much worse in your absence. The kids are still awake, wound up, eating sugary foods, and fighting furiously. Jane cut her leg tripping on the floor, and she's covered in blood. So, did checking out and ignoring the kids really help your health and stress levels? Probably not.

Babysitters are susceptible to germs and tantrums, too! As you have read, if you're watching little kids, you will likely have to deal with snot, vomit, urine, feces, and blood. These are very dangerous things, especially when you're stressed and making bad decisions. Here are some ways to keep yourself safe around kids.

Speak Up About Your Health

If you have chronic issues, like asthma, a weak immune system, or allergies, you should tell the parents. If you are sick with something temporary like a cold, they may not want you to sit. If they're aware of your condition, they can either ask you to take time off, or adjust your workload or environment accordingly. Maybe they'll vacuum up that dog hair before you come over, or maybe they'll ask the kids not to tax you too hard. If they don't know about your issues, how can they help you?

Take Necessary Precautions

Wash your hands frequently with soap and water, or with alcohol-based hand sanitizer, especially after you've handled saliva, diapers, dirty dishes, or anything germy. If you want to be extra safe, you  can wear rubber gloves when you're exposed to sickness, like when you're dealing with cuts. Also, be sure to stay healthy in general to keep that immune system strong. Eat a healthy diet, drink plenty of water, and exercise!

Prevent Sickness From Spreading

Curing an illness in its early stages is one surefire way to prevent it from spreading to you. If you notice that a child appears sick (coughing, vomiting, diarrhea, congestion, or scratching are telltale signs!), tell the parents immediately. They may suggest an over-the-counter medication or other cure.

Managing Stress

Not even Mary Poppins can deny that childcare is hard work. The stress can take a mental toll on the most hardcore, experienced babysitters around, but you need to stay in control if you want to keep the kids safe. It's totally natural to feel fatigued, angry, or downright annoyed with the children or the parents. But there are ways to maintain your sanity while also being a fun, safe sitter. If you are feeling particularly overwhelmed, slow down and count to ten. This is a surefire trick that will calm you down so you will be prepared for whatever comes at you.

① **Love your body.** While skipping a meal or staying up late before a babysitting job may not seem like a big deal, it could lead to dangers down the road. For example, sleep deprivation, low blood sugar levels, and dehydration can all make you feel dizzy, tired, or faint. This affects your ability to perform on the job, it clouds your judgment, and increases the likelihood of something bad going down.

② **Breathe deeply (and often).** It's easy to lose your cool when you're faced with loud screaming, nonstop crying, or constant defiance. Some situations can be so bad that you'll want to check out, walk out, and let the kids take care of themselves! Although it sounds cliché, taking a deep breath is a great way to calm your nerves before you reach your breaking point. Anytime you're feeling particularly anxious, stop what you're doing and inhale deeply through your nose. The full inhale should last for about ten seconds. Then, hold your breath for two seconds and let it all the air out in a big sigh. Keep repeating this breathing exercise until you feel your anger subside.

③ **Give yourself a break.** Just like parents who hire you so they can get time away from the kids, you need a break from your childcare duties, too. Make sure to leave plenty of space for your social life and interests, even if that means just blocking off an afternoon to veg in front of the TV. Regularly scheduled down time allows you come back to the job totally refreshed and ready to take on any babysitting challenge.

④ **Seek professional help.** If you're feeling perpetually stressed, frustrated, or depressed, it may help to get counseling. Your school or certified private counselor can help you sort out some tough feelings about your job. Whatever you do, don't let your frustrations fester. If you don't talk about on-the-job stresses with someone you trust, you may build up serious resentment toward the children, the parents, and babysitting in general. If you have no interest in the job, how can you protect the children?

⑤ **Know when to quit.** If the job is really making you go crazy, and none of the above stress tactics work, it may be time to quit. Just make sure to end the work relationship on a friendly note, no matter how angry or irritated you are. (See page 113 for advice on how to walk away.)

BUSINESS

BASICS

17. LANDING A JOB

You're a natural charmer. People seem to fall in love with you immediately. You're nice to all the kids in the neighborhood. You're polite to the adults. You're well-known for your community involvement. So, why hasn't anyone asked you to babysit their kids? Is it your breath? Chances are, no. The truth is, babysitting jobs don't always just fall in your lap, no matter how sweet you are. You have to be proactive. A lot of other people are hunting for babysitting jobs, too, so you have to appear professional and sell your skills in order to stand out. Here are seven steps to help you find that perfect babysitting gig and seal the deal.

Step #1: Create a Special Email Address

Before you start putting yourself out there, it's a good idea to create a separate email account that can be used strictly for babysitting purposes. This way, emails from potential clients and employers won't get lost in your already crowded inbox, and it's less likely that you'll make a silly mistake, like sending a stupid video of yourself to a child's parents when you intended to send it to a friend. Also, if your current email address happens to be something like Cutie555 or ILoveRobotz, employers won't take you seriously. Your professional email address shouldn't raise any eyebrows. You can use something babysitting-related like NYCsitter@yahoo.com, but if you can't think of anything clever, using your name is always a safe bet.

Step # 2: Prepare Your Résumé

A résumé is a simple way to highlight your babysitting background and skill-sets right off the bat, making it easy for a potential employer to see why you're perfect for the job. It should include your contact information, a one-line objective that sums up who you are and what kind of job you're looking for, past babysitting experience, and any additional skills that are relevant to childcare—think CPR certification, language fluency, or experience with special-needs children. You can also list your job as a coffee-shop barista or weed puller (it shows responsibility), but make sure there's plenty of childcare on there. Your experience should be listed in chronological order starting with the most recent gig, and it should include some details, like the ages of the children and the hours that you babysat. Don't worry if you don't have too many things to list. The entire point of a résumé is to keep things brief (ideally one page). And remember, caring for brothers, sisters, or cousins all count as experience! Check out the sample résumé on the next page and then try creating one on your own.

Sally Sitter
6 Caregiver Road
Kidland, NY 10000

OBJECTIVE:
Certified babysitter and entertainer looking for part-time work in the Kidland area.

EXPERIENCE:
2012: Part-Time Babysitter in Kidland, NY
Babysat for a 3-year-old and an infant after school until bedtime three nights a week.

2011: Part-Time Babysitter in Playville, NY
Babysat for an 8-year-old diabetic child on weekends for four hours a day.

2011: Part-Time Children's Entertainer in Kidland, NY
Guitarist/singer for children's birthday parties for Parties 'n Things Company.

EDUCATION:
Student at Kidland High School, Class of 2015
On the honor roll, on the basketball team, in the theatre department, and in the Key Club.

CPR Certification from American Red Cross, May 2012
Earned my Infant/Child and Adult CPR Certification

ADDITIONAL SKILLS:
Speak Greek fluently, guitarist/singer, basketball player, and actress.

Step #3: Choose Your References

Some employers may ask you for references. This probably means that they're interested in hiring you, but they want to talk to people you've worked for in the past to make sure you're as great as you seem. So if you have to give references, pick two or more former employers who you know will gush about you. Ideally, they should be able to talk about your childcare experience, your painstaking professionalism, and your glowing personality. (Don't pick the mean parent who complains about everything, including you.) If you don't have employment references, think of the other adults in your life—your teachers, your neighbors, and your coaches, for example. They can vouch for things like your promptness, your sense of humor, and your excellent character.

The new employer will probably want the phone numbers or email addresses of your references, so give your references a heads up before you hand over their information. You want to find out if these people even want to vouch for you, and it's common courtesy to let them know ahead of time that someone might be contacting them so they can be prepared.

Step #4: Talk to People You Know

The fastest way to get a babysitting job (or any job for that matter) is through people you know and trust. If you tell your friends and family that you're in the market, you may get a job quicker than you expect. Make a list of people you know who have kids. You probably know more than you think! Consider your family, your friends' parents, the people who attend your church or synagogue, and the parents at all your sports games or band concerts. Gather their contact information into one document, and spend a half hour each night calling them and sending emails. Tell them politely that you're looking for a babysitting job. If they don't need your services, maybe they know somebody who does.

If you already have some babysitting experience and are planning to make it a regular gig, you may also want to create business cards and advertise your services. (Skip ahead to page 116 to find out how.)

Step #5: Browse the Classifieds

Parents are constantly posting jobs on local online parent networks, as well as on websites like Sittercity.com and Care.com. So the job you want may already be out there, you just have to spend some time on the Web to find it. Of course, sorting through all the posts can get confusing, which is why it's helpful to know what kind of job you're looking for (you read Chapter 1, right?). Here are a few additional tips to help you get the most out of your browsing experience.

① **Look for details.** A good job ad includes the ages of the children, the babysitter's schedule, salary, and responsibilities up front. And all of these things should match what you had in mind. Also keep an eye out for any special considerations, like a language barrier, a disabled child, or transportation issues. If the parents include very little information, you should steer clear. Whatever their excuse, there are plenty of job listings with loads of helpful details.

② **Consider your qualifications.** Does the post specifically ask for a babysitter who is older than you? Does the child have special needs that you don't have enough experience to handle? Do the parents ask for CPR certifications (or other prerequisites) that you don't have? If the answer to any of these questions is Yes, don't apply. Stick to the jobs that suit your personal skills instead.

③ **Look for friendly language.** If parents insult their previous babysitters or sound bossy in the ad, imagine what they're like on the job! Parents should sound professional, friendly, and grateful for the help.

Step #6: Write a Winning Cover Letter

Found a job (or two) you like? It's time write a cover letter to include with your application. In the online world, a cover letter is an email message that's separate from your résumé and online profile. It's a way to speak to the employer, to express your enthusiasm, and to personalize your application so that your potential employer knows that you've thought hard about the job. Parents usually have to sift through tons of applications on online sites. If you don't include a cover letter, it's a good reason to overlook you.

On the next pages are two cover letters: a solid cover letter and one that could use a little work. Can you guess which one would land the job?

A. Tracey Sitter

tsitter@babysitting.com
September 24, 2012

To Whom It May Concern.

I am a qualified babysitter looking for work. I have three years of experience. I'm 16-year-old, and I live in Indianapolis.

You can contact me any time at tsitter@babysitting.com

Sincerely,
Tracey Sitter

B. Jeffrey Childs

jchilds@babysitting.com

Dear Mrs. Gomez,

I read your advertisement on Babysittingwebsite.com, and I'm really interested in babysitting for Miguel and Amy. I have experience with kids their age, and I think I would be a great match.

I've had three babysitting jobs in the Indianapolis area. During one part-time job, I babysat for a girl who is Miguel's age. I escorted her home from school, I helped schedule playdates, and I cooked her dinner three times a week. She wasn't a vegetarian like Miguel, but I'd be happy to learn new recipes.

I'm also great at coming up with fun play ideas. Like Amy, I play soccer. I also babysat for my brother when he was a baby, so I learned the art of playing imagination games like hide-and-seek for hours.

I'm 16-years-old, reliable, and prompt. I have access to a car if you need. I go to high school during the day, so I'm only available on evenings and weekends.

I hope you'll consider me for the job. I would be happy to provide any references, and I'm available for an interview upon your request.

Sincerely,
Jeffrey Childs

Sample A: Wrong! Cover letter A is missing a word. It should say, "I'm a 16 year old." Typos like this are common when you're typing, but it also shows the parent that you didn't care enough to check the letter for errors before sending. There's also no personal information or enthusiasm in the writing, and it looks like it was mass emailed to tons of different parents. The parents will probably wonder if Tracy Sitter even read the advertisement.

Sample B: Correct! Sample B has a personalized edge. It looks like Jeffrey Childs took a lot of time to consider the parents' advertisement. He used his qualifications to win the employer's heart, and provided some fun, kid-friendly information to show what kind of person he is. He's instantly likable.

Step #7: Nail That Big Interview

So you've made it to an interview. This means that the parents are already impressed with you on paper, and they want to get a sense of who you are in real life. During an interview, your personality can matter just as much as your qualifications. Parents want to see that you're mature, friendly, and on top of things. More important, they want to make sure you're a good match for their family. You want to bring you're A-game and let your great personality shine through. Here are some tips to nailing an interview.

① **Dress to impress.** You don't need to put on a suit when meeting parents for the first time, but you shouldn't look sloppy either. Instead, dress like you would on the job: comfortably (no high heels), modestly (no teeny shorts or low-cut shirts), and put-together

(no pajama pants or ripped shirts). You want your outfit to go relatively unnoticed so the parents can focus entirely on your personality.

② **Arrive prepared.** Show up five to ten minutes before the scheduled interview. You don't want to keep the parents waiting. Plus, arriving first gives you some quiet time to collect your thoughts, especially if you had to brave traffic (or a similarly chaotic situation) to get to the meeting location. Chances are, if you've made it this far, the parents have already seen your résumé. But it doesn't hurt to have one ready in a neat folder, and don't forget to list your references! You may also want to bring a notebook and pen so you can write down any extra details. This will make you look organized and serious about the job.

SAFETY FIRST!

Q. What if I'm worried about my safety?

A. The parents may seem perfectly nice through emails and phone calls, but they're still strangers. Suggest a public meeting place, like a restaurant or a park, for your first meeting. If they insist on meeting at their house, have a trusted adult drop you off at the house and pick you up later. If you have a funny feeling about anything, don't be afraid to bail. There are plenty of other jobs out there. Your personal safety should always come first.

③ **Be interested *and* interesting.** There's a misconception that interviews are all about talking. Actually, a good portion of an interview is sitting back and listening. Some employers are chatty during interviews. They want to talk about their kids, their jobs, their spouses, and some of them just want to gossip. While money may come up in the conversation, wait for the parents to bring it up. (For more on money talk, see page 104.) Ultimately, the parents want to get along with you, so try to appear easy to talk to. Of course, that doesn't mean you shouldn't talk at all. The parents probably want to hear about you, too. Not sure what to say? The following talking points can help:

- *Talk about one challenge you faced in a former job and how you fixed it.*

- *Tell one funny (but appropriate) story about babysitting.*

- *Share two (or more) fun facts about yourself, such as your musical skills or your Boy or Girl Scout merits.*

- *Ask at least three questions about the children that the parents didn't address in the job ad.*

- *Ask at least one question about the parents' jobs.*

④ **Tell the truth.** Be honest about your schedule and qualifications during an interview. For example, don't say you can work Fridays if you know you can't. Or don't say you're certified in CPR when you're not. You could wind up frustrating employers, or worse, seriously endangering a child.

⑤ **Be tolerant.** Keep in mind that families come in all shapes and sizes. Maybe they're more conservative than you. Maybe they observe religious diets that you don't. Maybe they have jobs that you don't morally agree with. If you want to babysit for a family that's different from you, you need to be tolerant of their background and ideals during the interview. Otherwise, tell them nicely that you have different beliefs, and perhaps you're not the best person for the job.

⑥ **Make a polite exit.** The interview is over when the parents say it's over. Parents may want to think it through before giving you a final decision on the job. Even if you're dying of anticipation, don't push them for an answer. Simply say it was a pleasure to meet them, shake their hands, and go home. You can follow up with a thank you email the next day. But now, the ball is in their court.

18. DECIDING HOW MUCH TO CHARGE

Figuring out how much money to ask for is one of the toughest parts of any job. It's particularly hard for babysitters because there are few set rules and laws to back you up. While some parents will say up front how much they're willing to pay, which would leave it up to you to

accept the rate (or not), it's still wise to have a price in mind. Here are several factors to consider when picking your pay.

① **The going rate.** On average, part-time sitters earn between $6 and $18 per hour. However, babysitting salaries also depend on where you live, so you'll want to do some research to find out how much your competitors are charging, especially those sitters with the same level of experience as you. You'll want to stay within this range so your rate doesn't seem totally out there.

② **Minimum wage.** In some countries (including the US) minimum wage is the lowest salary that employers can pay their employees. If they pay less, they're breaking the law. Minimum wage doesn't apply to part-time babysitters in the US and the UK, but it's still worth consulting your local salary laws to get some perspective. If the minimum wage in your city is $7 per hour, for example, it's probably reasonable to ask for anything between $5 and $12 for a babysitting job. Some helpful websites to check out are the United States Department of Labor site, dol.gov, if you live in the US, and direct.gov.uk if you live in the UK.

③ **The job expectations.** It's reasonable to charge parents more for additional responsibilities. For example, you could request $10 an hour for one child, $12 an hour for two, and so on. You may also be able to charge more than your usual rate for babysitting kids who require more care, like wheelchair-bound children. You should expect a bit of housework, like cleaning the dishes or cleaning up messes. But if the parents are asking you to go above and beyond, like mowing the lawn or mopping the floors, you should consider asking for more money.

④ **When to negotiate.** If an employer offers you an unreasonably low salary, you may be able to negotiate. And if you've worked with a family for a long time, they may be willing to give you a raise. Negotiating can be nerve-racking, but if you ask nicely and have convincing arguments, it might just work. Some good arguments include:

- *You're too qualified for the low salary.*

- *The job has too many responsibilities for such a low salary.*

- *You have been working the job for a long time.*

- *The salary is way below the standard minimum wage.*

TALES FROM THE CRIB

It was my first babysitting job and I was a timid sixth grader. I was hired by a family friend's mother. As I was young and new to babysitting, she asked me to watch the kids at a dinner party she was throwing. She said it shouldn't be too many kids and didn't mention the age range.

When I showed up on time for duty, there were fifteen kids, ages three to ten and a specific limited set of boundaries they could play in—two bedrooms. Terrified, I attempted to corral the little demons together. One was jumping from the top bunk of a bunk bed onto a beanie bag chair, while another sent hot wheels cars flying across the room. One was crying because she didn't get the Barbie she wanted as another took out every single board game available and threw around Monopoly money and the pink and blue people from LIFE. I guess you could say I had my hands full. As the three hours became four hours and the evening drudged on, my limbs became numb. I struggled to clean up the huge mess that was made by what one would think was a tornado, while counting heads every minute.

And the funniest part? When I was officially done and on my way out the door, I was handed a twenty-dollar bill: $5 per hour for four hours with fifteen kids. Let's just say that that night might have shaved a few years off my life.

— Annika, 14

19. KNOWING YOUR RIGHTS AND OBLIGATIONS

Most jobs offer a clear course of action for legal issues. For instance, a secretary can go to the human resources department to report sexual harassment. Or a doctor can go to the hospital's accounting department to complain about a missing paycheck. Babysitters, on the other hand, are working directly with parents in a home setting. And sometimes the rules aren't so obvious. But there are rules. Below are some ways to protect yourself from any legal issues and make sure you're following the law, too.

Your Rights

① **The right to a clear job description.** Parents should clearly outline the important details of the job, like the pay, the number of hours, and the number of days (if more than one) that you've agreed to work. The parents should also tell you what responsibilities you should expect, like picking up the kids from school, orchestrating a playdate, or cooking dinner. It's even better if the parents send these details in an email. That way, you'll have the job description in writing in case there is any confusion later.

② **The right to petty cash.** You should never have to pay for job expenses with your own money. If the kids are hungry, you shouldn't pay for groceries or takeout. If you drive the kids to school, you shouldn't have to pay for the gas, unless it's included in your salary. In general, the parents should leave you with cash for these things, or at the

very least, reimburse you at the end of the evening. If they forget to include the money with your regular pay, kindly let them know what you needed to buy while they were out, and how much it cost. Keep all of your receipts as proof.

③ **The right to a safe environment.** A broken staircase, the presence of toxic chemicals like pesticides or second-hand smoke, or major fire hazards like loose electric wires in a garage full of paper are all things you shouldn't have to deal with on a job. If the situation can be easily fixed, ask the parents to take care of it before you start working there. But if you think someone could get hurt, talk to an adult you trust about filing a complaint at your local health department. Of course, if there's a medical emergency or some criminal activity going on, you should call 911 right away!

④ **The right to quit.** If a job is not living up to your expectations, you have the right to quit. Obviously, you can't walk out on the kids while their parents are out. However, you can choose to not work for the family again. If you've already agreed to work for them long-term, it's common courtesy to give them enough time to find a replacement. Better yet, recommend a replacement to save them time. (See page 113 for more tips on quitting the job.)

Your Legal Obligations

① **To uphold your end of the deal.** Like the parents, you are also responsible for doing whatever it is you agreed to do. This is not only a good business practice, but you can also get fired if you don't uphold your end of the deal. So make sure you don't promise to do something if you know you can't deliver.

② **To keep the kids safe.** As soon as the parents leave the house, you are legally in charge of the children. You won't be arrested if they trip and fall, but there are ways to get in serious legal trouble. If you bypass your duties as a babysitter and the child is injured as a result, the parents can potentially sue you for negligence. For instance, if the child gets seriously hurt and you do nothing at all to help, or if you throw a party at the parents' house without permission and someone lights the place on fire with a cigarette, you could be charged with negligence. Here are some more important ground rules:

- *Don't show up intoxicated.*

- *Don't invite guests into the house.*

- *Don't take your eyes off little kids.*

- *Always call 911 in case of an emergency.*

③ **To pay your taxes.** In IRS land, babysitters are considered self-employed childcare providers, which means they have to pay taxes. If you make more than $400 in a year, you have to file a tax return using the form 1040. Consult your local tax laws and ask an adult about filing taxes.

20. UPDATING THE PARENTS

When the parents come home, you're still in business mode. Even though you're covered in food, disheveled, and exhausted, your professionalism is still on trial at this point. The few minutes after the parents arrive is your chance to show off your skills, prove that you're trustworthy, improve your performance, and maybe land more babysitting gigs. Once the parents have had a chance to settle in and check on their kids, wrap things up with these best practices.

Give Them the Good Stuff

First, tell the parents all the great things you accomplished. Did you cook dinner, invent a game, or put the kids to bed? Say so. Parents will be happy to know that they can trust you with these tasks.

SAFETY FIRST!

Q. How do I get home?

A. The most important thing is that you're safe. That should be your priority, the parents' priority, and the priority of your parents or guardians, too. Unless you live within walking distance in a very safe neighborhood, you should arrange a ride or escort in advance. Don't just expect a ride from your babysitting bosses unless you've already agreed on something. But if you're stranded without a ride and they seem completely unconcerned and unhelpful, you should probably think of getting another job.

Give Them the Not-So-Good Stuff

Also tell the parents about any loose ends. Apologize for leaving dirty dishes. Explain if the kids refused to eat their vegetables. Show them the vase that broke during an unruly round of hide-and-seek. Good babysitting bosses will respect your honesty, and may be able to offer advice for the future.

Show Off Your Bond

If the kids are awake, this could be a great opportunity to show off your new connection with them. Involve them in conversation in front of their parents. Ask them if they loved the green eggs and ham you made. And remember to give them a friendly goodbye.

Ask Leftover Questions

You'll probably have tons of questions when the parents come home. Is little Suzy's jaw clicking normal? Do you use baby powder? Is the backyard light supposed to flicker like that? This is the time to get answers to anything you were wondering about while you were on the job. And parents will likely appreciate your concern.

Handle Payments Efficiently

Do the math. Make sure the parents give you the correct amount for your wages and expenses. For extra assurance, you can type up an invoice with all your expense receipts attached. If they accidentally underpay you, politely inform them. If they overpay, you should give the extra money back. Hard as this may be, it will prove that you have excellent character.

21. KEEPING AND QUITTING A JOB

You're finally home. You've survived a successful babysitting gig and had fun while you were at it. Now, you breathe easy knowing there are no kids around. Is it over? Not if you want to be invited back. Alternatively, maybe it didn't go as well as you expected. The kids were crazy. You tried your best, you really did, but the fire alarms, endless crying, and inconsiderate kids proved to be a not-so-good fit. Here's what you should do if you want to keep or quit a job while still be professional.

Keeping a Job

To look like a pro even when you're off the clock, follow up each gig with a recap. The recap is a brief courtesy call (or email) letting the parents know that you really enjoyed your babysitting experience. You can also mention some of the fun things you did with the kids. It's a great way to seem eager for more work. Here's a sample recap that you can use as a model for your own:

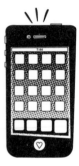

> Hello [insert parent's name],
>
> I just wanted to let you know that I really enjoyed my time with Johnny and Katie. No kid has ever beaten me at checkers before. You really have a wonderful family. Thanks so much for the opportunity! I hope to see them again soon.

Parents are busy, and they often take a while to respond. Sometimes there's not much more you can do except cross your fingers and hope for a call back. But if after a couple weeks you still haven't heard from Mom and Dad about a possible next time, try some friendly prodding like this:

Hello [insert parent's name],

I wanted to check in and see if you'll need my services next week, or later on. I had a great time with the family, and I wanted to see if I should make some room for you in my schedule. I look forward to hearing from you!

If the parents hire you back, respond immediately with a thank you. But if the parents give you the cold shoulder or tell you (nicely) that they won't need your services, try not to stress out. One rejection doesn't mean you can't babysit for other families. Mourn the loss for a few days, and be sure to handle any rejection with grace. You never know if the parents will change their minds. And you still want them to like you enough to recommend you to other families.

Here's a sample professional response to a rejection, just in case you need one:

Thank you for letting me know. While I'm disappointed, I'm glad I had to opportunity to meet your children. Please contact me any time if you change your mind in the future.

Quitting a Job

Maybe your first time working with a family was enough. Or maybe you've given it a few tries, and things aren't quite working out. Quitting a job is hard, especially when there are kids involved. But you shouldn't stick around out of guilt. And you shouldn't just end things without offering an explanation. Quitting is a lot like breaking up with a significant other. There's a nice way to do it. On the next page are some ideal ways to handle your escape.

Gather your reasons. People quit their jobs for a wide range of reasons, so you should have a reason, too. Take some time to think about why you're unhappy with the job. And be prepared to share those reasons with the parents. Some reasons may include:

- *You feel unsafe.*
- *It doesn't pay enough, and you can't negotiate with the parents.*
- *You don't have time to continue.*
- *You got another job.*
- *You're moving far away.*

Let them down gently. While it's important to be honest with parents about why you're no longer able (or willing) to work with them, remember to tell them your reasons without being harsh. Consider the parents' feelings throughout your conversation. Also give them plenty of notice so that they have time to find someone to replace you. For instance, if you want to quit because their kids are bratty, try couching it in something more polite, like this:

> *Hello [insert parent's name],*
>
> *I'm deeply sorry, but I'm afraid that I can no longer babysit for Lucas. I'm finding the job to be a bit too overwhelming. If you'd like, I can babysit for the next two weeks while you find somebody new.*

Refer someone you trust. If you can, recommend a trusted, qualified friend or acquaintance for the job (but be sure to tell you friend your reason for quitting the job). This shows the parents that you care about the job (and the kids' well being) even if you are quitting. Not to mention, it's often hard to find a replacement sitter right away, so parents will likely appreciate the help. Be sure, however, not to send your friend into a bad or dangerous situation.

Ask for a recommendation. If you left your babysitting job on good terms, keep in touch with the parents so they'll be willing to recommend you to other parents. One good way to keep in touch is to email the parents once in a while and ask about the children. Or stop by every once and a while for a visit (if it's appropriate). This will keep you fresh in the parents' minds so they can give you an excellent reference in the future.

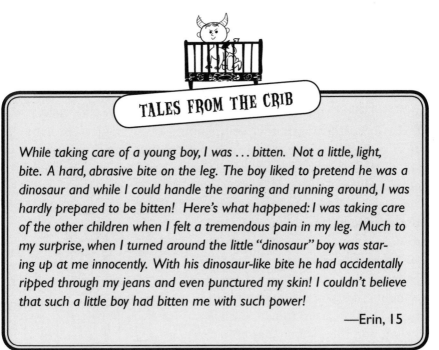

TALES FROM THE CRIB

While taking care of a young boy, I was ... bitten. Not a little, light, bite. A hard, abrasive bite on the leg. The boy liked to pretend he was a dinosaur and while I could handle the roaring and running around, I was hardly prepared to be bitten! Here's what happened: I was taking care of the other children when I felt a tremendous pain in my leg. Much to my surprise, when I turned around the little "dinosaur" boy was staring up at me innocently. With his dinosaur-like bite he had accidentally ripped through my jeans and even punctured my skin! I couldn't believe that such a little boy had bitten me with such power!

—Erin, 15

22. TAKING THINGS FURTHER

Are you thinking bigger? Now that you've racked up all these child-care qualifications, maybe you don't feel like going the traditional babysitting route anymore. If you're still serious about babysitting, but you want to take it further and make more money, there are lots of options out there.

Promote Yourself

Put yourself out there with professional advertising. It will help you garner clients, local buzz, and maybe even babysitting club members. These days, anyone can advertise with some pretty low-price methods.

Business cards. Business cards pack all of your contact information onto professional, wallet-size documents. Business cards are great for subtle advertising during conversations. If you overhear that your friend's parents are looking for a babysitter later on, you can hand them your swanky-looking card for future reference. Or if you overhear a mother complaining about the lack of baby-sitters in town, hand her a card to prove her wrong. You can also give your cards to your current clients to hand out to their friends and associates.

Posters/flyers. If you live in a safe, intimate community, you can post flyers that advertise your skills. Flyers are one-page, informal advertisements that you can post around town. They're cheap to make, fun to post, and there's a chance that your dream employer will see your

flyer and hire you. Be sure to post them in family-friendly locations where parents are likely to go, like restaurants, grocery stores, or libraries.

Online classifieds. Online advertising is really common among babysitters, and for good reason. A lot of job websites are free, and you can use them to reach thousands of parents without leaving your house. Make sure that you only post your advertisement on reputable sites (see your local Better Business Bureau to find out if a site has a good reputation!). Your odds are better if you advertise on more focused sites with an active babysitting section, like Sittercity.com, Care.com, Care4hire.org, or Babysitters.com. If you're looking for a specific client niche, you can join sites like Christianbabysitter.homestead.com if you're Christian, or j-sitter.com if you're looking for Jewish clients. Other sites, like Craigslist.org or Monster.com, are messes of thousands of jobs from every industry, so the babysitting section gets lost in the fold.

Website. If you build your own sleek page, clients will know that you're serious and very professional. It will also allow you to post all the information you want in one place without the restrictions of classifieds sites. If you want to avoid hosting and designer fees, you could also build a user-generated website, like on Facebook or Blogspot. These will enable you to interact with clients and update your site very easily. Just be sure to keep your professional page separate from your socializing page!

Team Up With Other Sitters

Teaming up with other babysitters is a great way to get lots of jobs without shouldering all of the work. You'll have help hunting for and taking jobs, and you won't be responsible for maintaining the business all on your own. You'll also be able to hang out with friends and voice your problems to people who understand.

Starting a club. To start a club, get dependable people working with you. Preferably, they should have plenty of babysitting experience, and maybe some experience with websites, advertising, or money management. Together, you can take turns garnering jobs, taking jobs, answering phones, running meetings, collecting dues, making the popcorn—however you choose to run things!

Starting an online babysitting group. If you don't have time for in-person meetings but you want to meet other sitters, you could start an online babysitting group. You could moderate a Facebook page, a personal website, or a blog forum where local babysitters can ask questions, post jobs, give advice, and build a community. If you get a good response, maybe this could lead to a bona fide club.

Look Into Other Jobs That Use Your Skills

If you love childcare but you don't want anything to do with baby-sitting anymore, you can use your qualifications to climb the ladder and apply for other jobs. (Some of them may pay more money, too.) If want to take your babysitting skills further, these are some jobs you can consider.

Camp counselor. Overnight or day camp counselors are in charge of multiple kids, sometimes for an entire summer. Some camps have entry junior counseling positions for teenagers.

Day-care worker. Day-care workers watch multiple kids while the parents are at work. These jobs are usually more official than private household gigs. Day-care workers usually work in a central office, and they need specific certifications to get the job. If you're looking to become a day-care worker, study up on your local day-care laws.

Tutoring. If you've done any babysitting for school-age kids, you've probably already done some level of tutoring. If you like tutoring, why not pursue it? Bone up on your subjects. You can even earn certifications to teach the ins and outs of standardized tests, like the PSAT.

Party services. Do you just like the "play" part of babysitting? You may be interested in working for a kids' birthday party service. You can try working as a clown, a magician, a children's song musician, an arts-and-crafts organizer, or any other fun entertainer position. Who knows, maybe you can start the biggest children's entertainment business in town.

Internships. If you're seriously interested in a childcare or an education career path, you should look around for an internship in your field of choice. Maybe you can intern in a school, a daycare facility, or a social work agency. Unfortunately, internships are usually unpaid, but you get unprecedented learning experiences, references, and a new shining star on your résumé.

Congratulations! You're on your way to becoming a star sitter. Now get out there and work! And don't forget to bring this handy guide with you—just in case.

Basic Training

Red Cross Babysitter's Training Course
www.redcross.org/takeaclass
Through this course, babysitters ages 11–15 can learn the basics, from landing an interview to handling emergencies.

Mayo Clinic
www.mayoclinic.com
The Mayo Clinic provides extensive and reliable medical information. From diaper rash to the flu, this site offers step-by-step instructions on how to recognize and handle illness. It also has information for handling tantrums.

US Department of Labor
www.dol.gov
If you're curious about things like minimum wage laws, babysitters' rights, how many people are babysitting or nannying in the world, the US Department of Labor is your best bet for accurate stats.

Parents Magazine
www.parents.com
Learn from the experts! *Parents Magazine* always comes with great advice for child care, including new recipe ideas, sleep issues, and fun holiday activities.

In Case of Emergency

Red Cross First Aid-CPR-AED
www.redcross.org/takeaclass
The Red Cross is the most reliable organization for First Aid and CPR. Get certified—it'll look great on the resume!

Poison Control Center
1-800-222-1222
If a child has ingested something toxic, call the poison control center immediately. Learn a jingle to commit it to memory: www.poison.org/jingle.

And remember, in the case of an emergency, if you are ever in doubt about what to do, or how to do it, always call 911 at any time.

Edu-tainment

PBS Kids
www.pbskids.org
PBS Kids is a reliable site for quality, educational games for kids ages 3–8. Plus, you might have some fun recognizing the characters from your childhood!

Sittercity's Compendium of Extraordinary Knowledge
compendium.sittercity.com
Sittercity is a widely respected babysitting job site—but, you need to be 18 to join. However, you can still benefit from Sittercity wisdom. The site's Compendium of Extraordinary Knowledge has loads of ideas for babysitting activities, from bubble print pop art to making faces on pancakes.

Kids Health
kidshealth.org/kid/recipes
This non-profit, expert site is not only an excellent source for information on illness—it also has great kid-friendly recipes! The site also includes recipe ideas for kids who are vegetarian, diabetic, or lactose intolerant.

Scholastic Homework Hub
www.scholastic.com/kids/homework
Is the kid getting frustrated with his homework? Scholastic offers free online help that *won't* bore kids to tears! The Homework Hub has fun quizzes, research tips, and study techniques in every subject.

Kids Know It
www.kidsknowit.com
This educational site for kids is full of astronomy, biology, dinosaur, geography, history, math, memory, and spelling games. It's a great resource for babysitters with kids who want internet time.

Nick Jr.'s *Yo Gabba Gabba!* Crafts Page
www.nickjr.com/yo-gabba-gabba
This site is full of crafts inspired by the hit kids show *Yo Gabba Gabba!*. Our favorite is the Shoe Box Puppet theater; print out the downloadable Puppet Theater backdrops and put on a show!

Halley Bondy is a Brooklyn-based writer who has worked as a news reporter for the *Newark Star Ledger*, an arts journalist for *Back Stage*, and as associate editor for *MTV Iggy*. She started babysitting as a teenager, joined the Barnard Babysitting Agency in college, and worked as a full-time nanny from 2007 to 2008.

To my parents, who were my first babysitters. To Tim, my current one. And to Dominik, my favorite little client.

NEW BOOKS FROM ZEST!

Junk-Box Jewelry
25 DIY Low Cost (or No Cost) Jewelry Projects
by Sarah Drew

The End
50 Apocalyptic Visions from Pop Culture That You Should Know About...before it's too late
by Laura Barcella

Scandalous!
50 Shocking Events You Should Know About (so you can impress your friends)
by Hallie Fryd

47 Things You Can Do for the Environment
by Lexi Petronis

How to Fight, Lie, and Cry Your Way to Popularity (and a prom date)
Lousy Life Lessons from 50 Teen Movies
by Nikki Roddy

87 Ways to Throw a Killer Party
by Melissa Daly

Freshman
Tales of 9th Grade Obsessions, Revelations, and Other Nonsense
by Corinne Mucha